T0062889

Mind
The Final Frontier

Mind

The Final Frontier

"DECODING THE HUMAN MIND"

RAVI SINGH

PARTRIDGE

To order additional copies of this book, contact
Partridge India
000 800 10062 62
orders.india@partridgepublishing.com

www.partridgepublishing.com/india

Contents

Acknowledgement

This book would not have been a reality without the inspiration and support of some people. I would like to begin by paying my respects to philosophers such as Shankaracharya, Immanuel Kant, David Hume and J. Krishnamurti from whom I have learnt a lot and more importantly realized that I am not the only one to have such 'weird' questions and ideas in my mind.

I would thank Sanjeev Sanyal, author of *Land of Seven Rivers* and Marianne Talbot, Faculty of Philosophy at University of Oxford for providing valuable inputs and suggestions.

I would like to thank my friends Anubhav Jha, Jai Sandhu and Subodh Chawla for providing useful suggestions and ideas.

I would also thank my parents for providing unconditional support to the endeavours I have taken in life including this one. They stand like a banyan tree under which I enjoy the freedom to play around.

Finally, I want to dedicate this book to my wife Neha without whose support I would not have the audacity to even think about writing this book. She was there to support and help me at each and every step of the process especially at times when I doubted myself.

Foreword

The mind, how it works, the ideas of 'self' and 'consciousness' have intrigued mankind for as long as the existence of humanity itself. As technology enables us to make greater inroads in understanding the human brain, a fierce debate rages amongst neuroscientists, psychologists and philosophers as they attempt to answer these questions.

In an age where humans are modelling machines on their own behaviour and to be more 'human-like', Ravi's book offers an interesting perspective on how the human mind can in turn be understood as a computer which processes information. With this approach he simplifies ideas such as self and consciousness while also helping in deal with practical problems of life such as fear, anxiety, boredom and even dealing with relationships.

His book strikes a chord in my heart. Throughout my life I've been asked how do I do so many things together. My reply to that question always is that I think of myself as a multitasking computer with a Unix kernel. A Unix kernel does many processes together by using round robin i.e. initiating many tasks in parallel and giving time to every processes regularly. With this method the computer is able to execute multiple tasks and it seems as if they are being done in parallel! That, I believe, is the secret to multitasking abilities.

For me, this perspective also raises an interesting question about what will happen if the two continue to converge – i.e. the human brain and machines. The questions of what is the mind, the self and consciousness might need to be answered all over again.

Coming from India, this book is also special because we're the birthplace of zero without which modern day computing would not be possible and of Sanskrit which is the most logical language for coding. Maverick thinkers like this may actually make India the birthplace of a new theory of evolution which is based on computing theory itself! Or of an artificial intelligence which is more human than humans themselves! The scope of this perspective is boundless – the idea of convergence of the human mind and machines in how they work may give rise to a lot more interesting developments and more philosophical or existential questions, not just for humans but maybe for machines too!

When I read the book written by Ravi, I found an overwhelming similarity of computing concepts to real world questions that we ask. It might not be the answer to a lot of questions that you want to know in the world, but we might discover the answer to a lot of them as 42.

It gives me pleasure and pride that a fellow engineering alumnus has written a book on such an important subject. He is an engineer turned consultant turned civil servant who's given a fresh perspective on an age-old philosophical conundrum. You should read this book if you want to answers to your questions and I wish Ravi the very best.

Vijay Shekhar Sharma

Founder, Paytm

Introduction

Two things fill the mind with ever new and increasing admiration and awe, the more often and steadily we reflect upon them: the starry heavens above me and the moral law within me.

**—Immanuel Kant,
Critique of Practical Reason**

Are you curious by nature? Do you think and introspect? What do you think about most often? Our minds are filled with all sorts of questions. Sometimes, we are primarily preoccupied with practical and day-to-day questions in life such as about the colour of shirt to wear to work tomorrow, ways to meet a stringent project deadline set by the boss, or options of birthday gifts to be given to a loved one, while at other times we are more concerned with abstract questions such as 'Who are we?' 'Where did we come from?' and 'Why we do what we do?' among other questions. Sometimes, we find answers to our questions and sometimes we don't. But instead of focusing on the contents of the mind, have you ever brought your attention to mind itself? Have you ever tried to understand what is the mind exactly and how it works? Although the mind is so eminently present, yet we often fail to recognize its importance in our lives. If it is understood properly, it cannot only help us lead better lives, but also help satiate our intellectual curiosity.

I have always been obsessed with and curious about the nature of reality and of life and about our place in it. Since my childhood, I have been troubled and intrigued by questions such as what is the purpose of life? Do we have free will? What is the self? How did the universe come into being? This inner urge has pushed me to look for answers everywhere. I have tried to understand such issues through the lens of physical sciences like physics and biology, social sciences like philosophy and psychology, religious texts, and also from everyday observations. Although these have helped in sharpening my understanding, my experience has led me to believe that ultimately, the answers don't lie outside but within us. For that, we must understand how the mind works.

Understanding how our mind works is the key to answering complex questions of life and reality. After all, it is only through mind that we *know* everything. But despite the great scientific breakthroughs in the past two centuries, I feel our understanding of the mind is inadequate. The reason behind this would be discussed in the first chapter.

It is normally assumed that you must have an academic background in psychology or philosophy to understand the mind. In fact, as mind is closely related to brain, it may also be assumed that one must be an expert on disciplines like biology and chemistry to understand the functioning of brain, and then one may have a chance of understanding the mind. I have always felt that there has to be a simpler and more intuitive way of understanding the mind without having expertise in any of the above disciplines. A basic knowledge of traditional disciplines, combined with common sense, should be sufficient to understand the mind and other abstract questions associated with it.

The eastern and western worlds have traditionally looked at the problem of understanding the mind very differently. I have tried to pick the best practices from both by using the scientific rigour of the west and the intuitive method of inquiry of the east. Based on the knowledge gained from several sources and self-inquiry, I have developed an understanding of mind that helps answer a lot of questions raised earlier. The intention is not to give a grand theory of everything that can answer all the questions conclusively; rather, it is to kindle the reader's mind and initiate them to ask the right questions about the several issues related to the human condition. Therefore, I have deliberately avoided using citations to keep things simple. It is a humble effort to tackle the complex questions of life by keeping *mind* at the core of my quest and extracting answers from this core. This book is intended for anyone who is intrigued by and interested in the fundamental questions about life and reality, and is willing to look for answers with an open mind. We live in a time where we have been conditioned in so many ways by the abundant flow of information around us. Thus, we must start from scratch without any preconceived notions to reach anywhere close to the answers.

The book has been divided in three parts. The first part of this book establishes a basic framework of mind based on a few assumptions. Some readers might find this part a little technical in nature, but I have tried to make it as simple as possible by using examples. Based on this framework, I have tried to explain ideas like self, consciousness, free will, conflict, expectations, etc. It is written from a philosophical perspective, which gives a lot of freedom as I can use my imagination liberally, but it also comes with a responsibility of adhering to logical consistency. The following parts are nothing but a logical extension and corollary of the basic framework.

In the second part, I deliberately enter the speculative realm and try to answer questions related to the nature of reality, God, love, etc. I must admit that in this part of the book, I have taken the liberty to rely more on my imagination, as the issues discussed are extremely abstract. The reader must also exercise his/her own intelligence before coming to a conclusion.

In the third part of the book, I come back from the realm of speculation to the practical life and discuss issues that concern our daily lives like relationships and job satisfaction. Parts two and three are based on the framework established in part one. One needs to be careful when reading part three. The terms used in this part like the *self* may have been differently understood in part one. But to keep things simple, I have stuck to the colloquial meaning of the terms used here, as this is the best possible way to convey the ideas at the practical level.

The tone of the book is more descriptive than prescriptive because there are no absolute rights or wrongs; rather, there is less understanding and more understanding. In fact, this is a recurring theme in the book (i.e., the focus on understanding and not merely theorizing). An example can help make things clearer. A lot of people are afraid of the dark. Instead of fighting that fear, if it is understood properly, it will automatically dissolve. Thus, the approach here is to improve our understanding and then see what follows. We are on the same ship, and the idea is to explore the vast sea called mind together. It is commonly believed that space is the final frontier of our quest for knowledge and truth, but I believe the place to look for answers does not lie outside us, but within us and thus mind is the final frontier.

So with the focal centre as the mind, let us begin our journey towards the final frontier.

> *Reality exists in the human mind and nowhere else.*
>
> *—George Orwell, 1984*

PART I:

Decoding the Anatomy of Mind

We are all in search of feeling more connected to reality—to other people, the times we live in, the natural world, our character, and our own uniqueness. Our culture increasingly tends to separate us from these realities in various ways. We indulge in drugs or alcohol, or engage in dangerous sports or risky behaviour just to wake ourselves up from the sleep of our daily existence, and feel a heightened sense of connection to reality. In the end, however, the most satisfying and powerful way to feel this connection is through creative activity. Engaged in the creative process we feel more alive than ever because we are making something and not merely consuming, masters of the small reality we create. In doing this work, we are in fact creating ourselves.

—Robert Greene

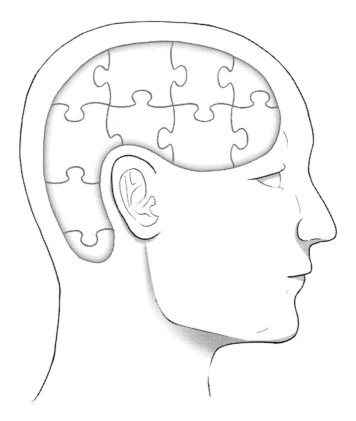

Mind Games

Trying to define yourself is like trying to bite your own teeth.

—Alan W Watts

When was the last time you used Google to know about something? Was it yesterday, today, or in the last one hour? Google has been so successful because it provides answers to our questions. We are always looking for answers. We do so because we are curious by nature. Curiosity has been one of the biggest drivers of our civilization. People have risked their lives looking for answers. If it was not for curiosity, Columbus would not have discovered America, Copernicus wouldn't have discovered earth's position in the solar system, Darwin would not have discovered the principle of natural selection, Newton would not have discovered gravitation, Alexander Fleming would not have discovered penicillin, and Mendeleev would not have formulated the periodic table. It is curiosity that pushes us to move out of our comfortable lives and investigate the world around us to find answers. Most children ask a lot of questions, which indicates how hardwired are we to be curious. But the questions given birth by curiosity fall in two very different realms: the external and the internal. The questions about the former pertain to physical objects lying outside us, whereas those about the latter pertain to the realm of the mind. While our inquiry of the former leads to questions such as 'why does it rain?', 'why is the colour of the sky blue?', 'why do we fall sick?', 'what is water made of?' etc., that of the latter leads to questions such as 'who am I?', 'what is consciousness?', 'what is it like to be happy?', 'what is the right thing to do?' etc. There is a vast difference between the methods of inquiry in both the realms.

Inquiry and observation of the external world is based on the assumption that there is an object to be studied and a subject, which studies that object by observing, hypothesizing, experimenting, and theorizing. For example, we observe that when we throw a ball vertically upwards, it comes back downwards. We ask the question, why does it come back and not keep going up? Based on this observation, we intuitively formulate a hypothesis (i.e., there must be a force that brings the ball down). To test this hypothesis, we perform experiments under controlled conditions and record the results. If these results are in consonance with our hypothesis, we formulate a theory. This theory helps us in answering our question. Newton would have followed similar steps to formulate the theory of gravitation. The knowledge thus obtained is objective in nature, as it can be validated and verified by others by repeating the experiments. Here, Newton would have been the subject and the ball the object.

For studying the mind, however, the object of study is the subject itself. This means that it is very difficult to conduct experiments and record observations on the mind in the same way as we do for external objects. It is like measuring a scale with that very scale.

Although with the advancements in disciplines like neuroscience, it is now possible to study the brain more objectively than ever before, but it still fails to address questions such as who am I and what is consciousness? Thomas Nagel, in his famous paper, 'What is it Like to Be a Bat?' states that '*it seems unlikely that any physical theory of mind can be contemplated until more thought has been given to the general problem of subjective and objective.*' It needs to be made clear here that we intend to understand the 'mind' in its broadest sense, and are not concerned with its direct relation to the brain.

One may ask why is it important to know how the mind works? Is it merely an intellectual exercise or it has any bearing on day-to-day life? As the majority of the population across the world is moving toward a materially prosperous life, we have come to realize that material comfort might be a necessary condition for happiness, but it is by far not the sufficient condition. There is still a significant segment of the world's population reeling under poverty, but it is also true that the 'well off' segment of the population is facing 'first world problems' like loneliness, anxiety, depression, etc. Most of these problems may have their cause and remedy in how we understand the functioning of mind.

Now arises the question, how do we get inside our own minds? When I commenced my quest to answer questions about the self, the mind, consciousness, etc., I tried multiple routes. I studied a variety of subjects such as biology, physics, chemistry, mathematics, and social sciences in search of answers to my questions. I even thoroughly went through various religious texts. I even meditated a lot and still do till date. All these disciplines had something or the other to offer. Sometimes, I would get a glimpse of my answers in the elaborations of a single subject or a conjunction of some subjects taken together. There might have been other important learnings from such subjects, which I might have completely missed out of oversight.

Somewhere down the line, I stumbled upon an approach, which was not only flexible enough to accommodate the essence of all such disciplines, but also provided something more than their sum that I could use to augment my understanding of the mind—The Information Processing Approach.

Thus, I present here a model of the mind, which uses the Information Processing Approach (IPA) that has been used in cognitive psychology before. It is a representation of reality and not reality itself. But it helps in understanding reality in a better way. It assumes that individuals are information processors and have similarities with computers in the way information is handled by them. After laying the foundations of how the mind functions using IPA, I will try to explain the ideas like self, consciousness, time, conflict, etc.

Game of Names

Imagine if there were no names in this world. How would you call out a companion, or how would you ask for a particular thing? Fortunately, we humans are blessed with a unique ability—the ability to abstract. While sense organs are windows to reality, the sense data received by these sense organs is collected, organized, and named based on certain rules. This is called abstraction. It is a representation of reality and not reality itself. We name objects based on their common properties; for example, the sense experiences of roundness and redness (sight) and sweetness (taste) are abstracted into an idea the name of which is apple. It helps us in making sense of the world around us.

We use abstraction not only to name objects but also to understand the relations between them. For example, the gravitational force is an abstraction of how two objects attract each other. Similarly, the atomic theory is an abstract model to understand how entities like electron, proton, and neutron function at the fundamental level.

Several famous theories from the areas of science and technology including gravitational theory were initially proposed as abstract models. Later, they were validated using observations obtained from relevant experiments. But for theories pertaining to concepts like the mind, it might not be possible to validate the model using physical experiments.

Rather, the theory can be validated if it is logically coherent (does not transgress its own assumptions) and by internal observations. By internal observations, I mean observation of the mind made by the subject. This obviously leaves scope for subjectivity as people might observe their minds subjectively, but it is unavoidable. I can assure you that the dots would connect in the end.

Other examples of abstract models include Einstein's theory of relativity (nobody has 'seen' the space-time curvature), programming algorithms in computer science, Kant's transcendental deduction, Shankaracharya's Advait Vedanta, etc.

Mind Modelling

Now that we understand what abstraction means, we need to ask ourselves the question: what is it that lies behind this word called 'mind'? Is it the brain, is it the software running the body, is it the intelligence of a person, or is it something else? Now, if we ask a hundred people across different cultures and nationalities, we might receive a hundred different answers. In order to proceed then, let us dispel any preconceived notions about the mind, and agree that we do not know what the 'mind' is. That should be a good starting point.

Also, since nobody has physically seen the mind, let us be clear that we are attempting to create a model of the mind based on indirect observations. It is similar to the model of the earth's crust we created based on seismic waves received from it and radio waves reflected by it.

Going forward, we need to outline the contours of our study of the mind for which we need to lay down some assumptions. The first and foremost assumption here is that we are considering the mind to be an information processor. Now, it may be tempting to question the assumption itself, but let us refrain from doing so at this stage, and let us try to understand the hypothesis.

Another piece of advice here—the content in the next few pages might seem a bit technical and difficult to comprehend, but it is important to grasp some basics to start with in order to build upon them further. Think of it like a Nolan movie, which seems a bit slow and technical at first, but builds upon its initial part for a nail-biting

9

climax and revelation. Only when you see the whole picture together will it make sense.

Now let us dive into the core of the Information Processing Approach model. First, let us start by asking what information is. Is it the gigabytes of movies on your computer, the tonnes of books in a library, or is it something else?

Here, it means any information reaching an individual, which is capable of being processed by him/her. It is to be understood in the broadest sense. For example, sound waves travelling through air carry input information. Light signals reaching the eyes of an individual is also input information. At the finer level, thoughts are also input information.

So what happens when such information reaches a person?

An individual receives input information either from external environment or from internal memory (referring to the function and not a physical entity like a computer hard disk) through an interface. This input information is processed by a specific processor(s) to produce a change in the individual. This change acts as input information for another processor and so on and so forth. This change is physical in nature, and thus, it is in accordance with the philosophical position of physicalism.[1]

---

1   Physicalism means that everything is physical, and there is no any other kind of *substance*. Some religions and schools of philosophy believe there are fundamentally two kinds of substances—mind and matter—and they are qualitatively different. A commonly quoted example by these schools of a

What do we mean by 'interface' here? Think of a dish antenna at home, which receives information from broadcasters and sends it to your television. An interface is the place where a certain kind of input information is received. For example, ears are the interface for sound waves, and eyes are the interface for light waves.

What do we mean by 'processor' here? Think of a computer program, which performs the operation of adding numbers. When it receives an input of different numbers, it automatically adds them and provides the sum as an output. This sum of numbers may further be used as input by another computer program, which performs a different operation. Similarly, processors here refer to a set of instructions to be performed over input information of particular quality and range. For example, when sound waves from the external

---

non-physical entity is the soul. But I assume here that every process including mental processes is essentially physical in nature. They might be gross or subtle, but they are grounded in a physical process. The subtle ones might seem to be non-physical. So if you are thinking about your dinner tonight, there is a physical process behind the thought that involves your skin, muscles, neurons, hormones, etc. Every mental activity can be mapped to a physical process in the body e.g. firing of group C nerve fibres is commonly correlated with pain. You might not agree with such an assumption, which is fine, but I request you to be patient and accept these assumptions as the starting point for the time. In the second part of the book, we will see how physicalism may be inadequate in explaining several phenomena.

environment enter the ears, they are first processed by a processor, which organizes them based on pitch and loudness. The next processor processes this output and abstracts the information to produce words of a language. These words are then organized into sentences based on language semantics. We must understand that a processor has to be understood as mental construct. It is an abstract entity.

What do we mean by 'change' here? We are not referring to the commonly understood meaning of the word here. Think of the pang of fear you would feel on seeing a snake close to you. It is caused by the release of the hormone adrenaline triggered by the input visuals received by your eyes—the release of hormone is the change we are referring to. When input information is processed, it produces a change in the individual. This change may be chemical, physical, electrical, etc. Some changes might be more potent than others. More potent changes could express themselves through behavioural manifestations. These changes of whatever nature or potency act as input information for another processor. The change may give the individual a sensation or a feeling.

Now that we have established the foundation of the model, let us get to the interesting part.

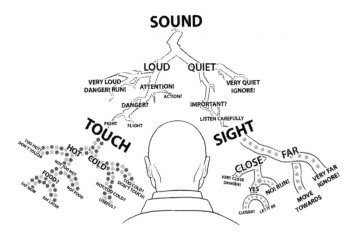

Mind at Work

Functioning of Mind based on Information Processing Approach (IPA)

> The mind is the most capricious of insects—flitting, fluttering.
>
> —Virginia Woolf

Now let us try to understand in detail how our mind works based on how it processes information. How does the mind receive input information? It can receive information through six channels or *interfaces*—the five sense organs: eyes, ears, nose, tongue and skin, and the internal memory. The input information received is processed by one of the processors.

Imagine yourself sitting in a quiet room. There is a TV in the room behind you. Somebody turns on the TV. There is a song coming, which happens to be one of your favourite songs. You become happy and nostalgic hearing it. What exactly has happened here? Let us slow down the flow of time a little bit and see closely.

Stage 1

As soon as the song started playing, the TV speaker started vibrating the air molecules near it. Those molecules created vibration in nearby molecules and so on and so forth until the vibration reached your eardrums. The eardrums detected the pattern of vibration.

This is the first level of information processing done by our body/mind. We cannot control this processing of information. Two important points need to be noted here:

- A particular kind of information, in this case sound vibrations, although reach all the five external sense organs, but are processed by only one—the ears. For the other sense organs, the information is inert.

- We are in a sense hardwired to process it. The sound vibrations detected by our ears act as input, get processed, produce a change, which acts as an input for the next information processor. We cannot prevent the raw sound from getting converted into a familiar song.

This is an evolutionary phenomenon. During the process of evolution when organisms were 'developing' auditory organs, it helped them in their survival as they helped in identifying a predator from a distance. This was so elementary and indispensable for survival that it was hardwired in animals including humans over millions of years and is intact even today.

Stage 2

Coming back to the song, once the ear processes the sound vibrations, the output serves as input to a particular faculty of mind, which can be treated as an input by the next processor. Here, the pattern of vibration gets matched with a pattern of vibration already present in the memory. This process of comparison and matching is also involuntary. If the input pattern matches with a pattern belonging to a language, which you know, the vibration patterns would be organized based on the syntax and rules of that language.

Stage 3

In this stage, the particular vibration patterns of words and sentences would be looked into the memory for their individual and combined meanings. This will act as input for the next stage processors. In this case, as you like this song, the *change* produced by the processor would cause a sensation of pleasure.

The stages of processors are not so discrete and sequential. There can be many stages in between; for example, before you process a sound vibration for language information, you might process it through a more basic processor, which is sensitive to pitch and intensity of the vibrations. Had the volume of the TV been very high before realizing what song it is, you would realize that the sound is very loud. But for the sake of understanding and developing a theory, we will call these processors as *basic or low-level* processors and the processors at the above three stages can be conceptualized as the following:

Stage 1: Abstraction processor: makes rudimentary distinctions like high and low, big and small, near and far

Stage 2: Language processor: organizes the sound waves based on the rules and syntax of a language

Stage 3: Pain-Pleasure processor: attempts to minimize pain and maximize pleasure

The low-level processors are the building blocks of our mind and have been so fundamental in our survival that they seem to be hardwired. In the above example, the sequence of processing was in this order only. But in other cases, they might follow a different sequence. For example, if you sprain your ankle while running, the pain-pleasure processor will kick in first followed by the other two. Thus, I will reiterate here that these processors are mental constructs and need not follow a particular order in processing information.

Range and Quality of Information

Imagine a packet of information arriving at the gate of an interface wearing a badge, which reads its range and quality. Example of badge:

Quality – Sound Wave   Range – 200 Hertz

Just as our eyes are programmed to process visual data and ears to process sound data, every processor is programmed to process a particular *range and quality* of information. Light waves would be inert for the ears. If the input information falls in that limit, it will automatically be processed by that processor. If not, the input information would be inert to that processor. This will be significant when we will try to understand high-level processors.

Before moving beyond Stage 3 processors, let us look at another example of information processing. If you were to face the TV, you would also be getting visual data in your eyes through light. As our ears are programmed to process sound vibrations in a particular way, our eyes are also programmed to process data in a certain way.

The raw light data first enters the eye. It is then processed through the pupil, the iris, and the retina. The recorded wavelengths are looked at and matched with the wavelength present in memory. Based on this, the next processor processes information with outputs like colour and size specifications. Then these abstractions are given names based on memory.

This process too is very involuntary as it has been hardwired in organisms over millions of years as it has helped in survival.

Chain Reaction

Relation Between Input and Output

If I prick your arm with a pin, you will react by moving your body away from the pin. This is a simple case of how an input sensation produces a change (output), i.e., you moving your body. Sometimes, you can control (or at least it appears so) how you process the input sensation and your ensuing reaction and sometimes you cannot.

The functioning of mind can be understood as a chain of input information and corresponding output sensations. If an input sensation falls in the range of an information processor, it gets processed by it, yielding an output, which may act as input for another processor of corresponding range.

So when I prick your arm with a pin, the input information is processed by a particular processor (for instance, *pain-pleasure processor, among others,* as it has the particular range). The output is a behavioural reaction to avoid pain, which has been hardwired into us. Pain is a critical survival skill. Had we not felt pain during our evolution, we may not have survived as a species.

But if I pinch you a little lightly, you may 'choose' to react in a particular way. The input information does not quickly pass through a processor initiating a *change*, which moves your body involuntarily. In this particular case, how much you can choose will be discussed later.

Up to the lower stages, the processors corresponding to input information are very basic and strong. What do we mean by basic and strong? They are basic because they are very old, maybe millions of years old (e.g., the ability to differentiate between big and small would have developed quite early in the chronology of evolution, we humans have simply inherited it from our ancestors) and they process rather crude data. They are strong because they have been reinforced intensely through repetition over many times. They process information (of their quality and range) so fast that we don't even realize it. Can you look at a sentence of a language familiar to you, and not *read* it? As we move from lower stages to higher stages, the strength of the processor goes down, as the latter are comparatively newer habits. At the cost of oversimplification, let me say, if the lower stage processors are millions of years old, higher stage processors may range from thousands of years old to a few seconds old.

is an overlap in both quality and range of information being handled by them.

Another difference from the low-level processors is that they are comparatively weaker and can get altered in our very lifetimes relatively easily. This gives a sensation that we have a choice to react in a certain way to a particular input sensation. It is not as involuntary as the pain-pleasure processor, but that doesn't in any way indicate that we have complete control over them (more on this ahead, hold on!). Even among the high-level processors, the processor, which is older, will be stronger than the one that is comparatively younger.

Let's go back to the TV example again.

You listen to the song, and you don't even realize the process in which that air vibration reaches one of your thought processors. Now it happens to be one of your favourite songs. As soon as the sound vibration is matched with your favourite song wavelength in memory, the output, which acts as input sensation for one of your thought processors, gets processed. You get a pleasant sensation because in your memory, it is associated with pleasure. If it is an old processor (i.e., if memory of the song is associated with childhood and/ or it has been reinforced over the years), the pleasant sensation is almost involuntary. If it is recent, it is less involuntary.

If for the same input information, the strengths of some processors are comparable, we might have two or more outputs, and we might feel that we have a choice to react in a particular way. We might think that we can exercise control over which processor can be allowed to dominate. The relatively stronger processor will however decide the final reaction. But since these processors are not very strong (unlike low-level processors), their strength would alter based on other factors like external environment, physiology, or basically 'the state of mind.' If such a situation repeats over a period of time, there might be creation of a new processor, which will decide the reaction next time based on how the input was handled in the past.

For example, if I come across an extremely tempting piece of cake on my table (while I have a full belly), two types of thoughts may cross my mind. First, since the cake looks delicious, I should eat it; and second, since the cake is loaded with extra calories, which are bad for my health, I should not eat it. We might feel that we have the power to decide whether or not to eat the cake. Practically, however, one of the processors will dominate depending on a host of factors, which may collectively be termed as 'state of the mind' without any control from our side. You might disagree at this stage, but we will discuss this in much detail in further sections.

Cast from Past
Meta-Processors

We have already discussed low-level processors such as abstraction, language, and pain-pleasure. These are also meta-processors. Since they are the oldest and most fundamental processors, the high-level processors are their derivatives, and thus carry their characteristics to varying degrees. No matter which thought comes to our mind, it will always have the characteristics of abstraction, language, and pain-pleasure processors. Their degree may vary, but no thought is possible without them. Thus, they are called meta-processors. They can be used to explain other kinds of feelings and sensations. Broadly speaking, we may compare meta-processors (which are primitive and basic processors) with the colours red, green, and blue. Just like every colour contains varying degrees of RGB elements, every high-level processor borrows from meta-processors in varying degrees and proportions.

To substantiate this, let us reconsider the cake example with a slight variation. You are reminded of the piece of cake you had seen lying on your table through a thought. In your thought, you recognize it as something edible and tasteful through the meta-processors of abstraction and language. You might even say to yourself, 'What a tempting cake.' Further, the thought of eating it is based on the meta-processor of enhancing immediate sensory pleasure, and the thought of not eating it is based on the meta-processor of reducing future pain of an unhealthy body.

Time Scale of Processors

Processors are a result of past habits and experiences—some very old and some recent. Thus, they can be put on a time scale:

Time scale of the creation of Processors

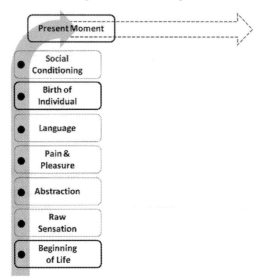

Illustration 2.1

Illustration 2.1 shows different processors on the time scale. The processors at the bottom are the oldest, and thus are the strongest. They process information at lightning speed, and thus seem involuntary. As we move upwards on the time scale, the processors are younger and weaker compared to their earlier counterparts. The processing speed of processors becomes slower as we move from left to right. The younger processors are derived from the older processors (external environment also plays a role here), and thus share their characteristics. One might question the positioning of language processor before the birth in the time scale. This is a valid question. But it needs to be emphasized here that we are talking about the processors associated with language, and not the actual use of language. It is now widely accepted by linguists like Chomsky that we are born with genetic structures that help us in learning a language.

Thus, we always look at things from the lens of the past. The input information is processed based on processor, which is based on past habits.

Self: Am I?

For my part, when I enter most intimately into what I call myself, I always stumble on some particular perception or other, of heat or cold, light or shade, love or hatred, pain or pleasure. I never can catch myself at any time without a perception, and never can observe anything, but the perception. If anyone, upon serious and unprejudiced reflection thinks he has a different notion of himself, I must confess I can reason no longer with him. All I can allow him is that he may be in the right as well as I, and that we are essentially different in this particular. He may, perhaps, perceive something simple and continued, which he calls himself; tho' I am certain there is no such principle in me.

—David Hume

What is the self? Is it the mind or the body, or both or neither? Is it temporary or permanent? These have been some of the most pertinent questions in the history of mankind. According to Buddhism and philosophers like David Hume, there is no permanent entity like the self. According to Bhagvad Gita, there is a permanent soul, but it is quite different from the idea of self normally envisaged. How can 'self 'or 'I' be explained using the Information Processing Approach? Ideally, we should start with the basic question, 'What is the self'; but we will come to it later.

First, let us ask the question whether 'self' is temporary (ephemeral) or permanent. You met a person ten years ago when he was fifteen years old, and you meet him today. Is he the same person or different? His physical appearance has changed, and his way of thinking has also changed. Yet, there is some similarity between the older and the present versions of the person. This problem has been addressed by many philosophers in the past. Let us try to understand it using Information Processing Approach.

We have discussed that low-level processors process information involuntarily and how it is processed varies across individuals. Therefore, even as a person grows up, the way low-level processors would process information will not undergo much change. Let's start with stage 1, he will process sound vibrations in a particular way based on his physiology (and genes). At stage 2, the vibrations would be associated with a language as the case may be. At stage 3, he will make sense of the noise. Till this stage, whatever information processing takes place is largely involuntary, and the output would depend on genetic making of the person. This will give a sense of 'permanence' about the personality of the 'self' of the person.

Now, as we move to processors above stage 3, they undergo change based on environment and habit as the person grows up. His world view would change, and accordingly, his conception of the 'self' would change. Thus, the high-level processors would be responsible for giving an impression of 'non-permanence' about the person's self.

But if in an entity, some parts are permanent and some are changing, we would not call the whole entity permanent; rather, we will call it non-permanent. In fact, even the low-level processors are not a hundred per cent permanent.

Thus, from the perspective of Information Processing Approach, the notion of self is non-permanent, which brings us to back the basic question itself 'What is self?' Or 'Who am I?'

Who am I?

'I' is a conception (an abstraction or symbol of reality) and is determined by the 'state of mind' at a given moment of time. We will come to what is state of mind, but first we must understand 'I' is not a permanent unchangeable entity sitting inside our minds.

If somebody pricks a pin in your arm, you react by removing your arm away from the pin. Do you do it voluntarily or involuntarily? Can you say that 'I' removed my arm when the pin was pricked? Did you actually have a choice? If we push a chair, it gets pushed. Can an observer say that the chair felt the push, and thus it moved?

When there is a behavioural manifestation of the output coming from a low-level processor (e.g., pain-pleasure processor in the case above), there is no feeling of 'I' at that moment. In this case, the high-level processors are not involved, as there is no 'thought' taking place. You might have thoughts after the event.

Now let us see what happens to 'I' when high-level processors are involved. As we have discussed before, when high-level processors are active/involved, there might be more than one output possible for a single input sensation. For e.g., if you see a chocolate cake in front of you, the image and fragrance of the cake is processed through the low-level processors and reaches the thought level. At this level, you have processors, which are young and relatively weaker. For our convenience, let's take two processors:

- P1: It processes the input information and releases chemicals, which give a sensation of craving for the cake.

- P2: It processes the input in such a way that you get the sensation: I should not be eating this as it has a lot of calories.

Both the processors are capable of processing the input information (because of their quality and range).

There is a *competition* between the two processors. As a result, you get the feeling of 'I should eat the cake' or 'I should not eat the cake.' Here, the 'I' is nothing but the sensation created by the 'change' produced by one of the processors.

It can be understood by the analogy of a CD player. Consider the different CDs as the processors. As we put one CD on the player, it starts playing. If the CD is of a jazz artist, the player might think it is a jazz singer. If we change the CD to pop, the CD player will think it is a pop singer. Similarly, based on the thought processor, which is more active, we think we are that. There is no such thing as a permanent or non-changeable 'I'. But if the CDs are changed very quickly, the system would feel it could sing in its unique genre and that is its permanent identity.

Similarly, the thought processors are so active and unstable that at one moment, one processor is active and producing an output sensation; and at the next moment, another is active. This 'state of mind' gives a cumulative sensation of 'I' in a particular context and time.

Thus I, or self, is also an abstraction of reality. It represents reality and is not reality itself. It is also conceptualized using the meta-processors (i.e., abstraction, language, and pain-pleasure). The conception of 'I' at a particular moment of time would depend on the state of mind.

'State of mind' depends on the following factors:

- Consciousness
- Physiology
- External environment
- Past conditioning

Thus, the sensation of 'I' can be seen as ephemeral or permanent depending on the consistency of above factors.

The more fragile a processor is, the more it would be affected by the factors on which state of mind depends. Very often, we experience that when we are in a good mood, we see things positively, and when we are in a bad mood, we see things differently. This mood is nothing but a manifestation of state of mind. The state of mind determines the strength of a processor, its range, and stability.

A similar view on self is shared by Buddhism. According to Buddhism, the self is simply a dynamic aggregate of five skandhas(groups): form, feelings, perceptions, impulses and consciousness. There is no distinct substance known as the self. Buddhist sage Nagasena explained this beautifully to King Milinda in second century BCE using the example of a chariot. Just as 'chariot' is used to describe a combination of various parts like wheel, axle, framework, etc similarly 'self' is used to describe the combination of the five skandhas. It doesn't have an independent existence outside its parts.

Consciousness:
Pervasive yet Elusive

We are the cosmos made conscious, and life
is the means by which the universe understands
itself.
—*Brian Cox*

Consciousness has been a key area of study in various fields of inquiry like philosophy, biology, neuroscience, etc. Over the years, scientific advancements have helped us in understanding the physical processes taking place when we are conscious of something. It is now known that certain parts of the brain get activated when we are performing an activity. For example, listening to music activates the motor cortex. But the understanding of consciousness itself is very limited.

For understanding consciousness, what should be our starting point, and where should we head toward from there? Let us start with a mental state where there is no consciousness. Can you think of such a state? When we are awake, we are always conscious of something. When we are asleep, we are conscious in our dreams. But if we are sleeping and not having any dreams, are

37

we conscious? I don't think so. Thus, such a state exists in dreamless sleep. In this state, there is no processing of information by high-level processors. Thus, 'no consciousness' *is the state when there is no processing in the high-level processors.* Of course, there will still be processing occurring in low-level processors for the various body systems, like respiratory and digestive systems, to function.

When we are in wakeful state, there is processing taking place in at least one of the high-level processors. Thus, *conscious state is the state where one or more high-level processors are processing information and producing corresponding changes in us*. It is the state of being conscious of something.

We know from our experience that there are degrees of consciousness, which varies at different points in time. Sometimes, we are more conscious than at other times. When we just wake up in the morning, we are less conscious; but as the day progresses, we become more conscious. The degree of consciousness is determined by the physiology, conditioning, and the external environment. In fact, these factors determine the size of the *window of consciousness*.

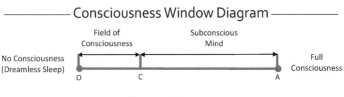

——————— Consciousness Window Diagram ———————

	Field of Consciousness	Subconscious Mind	
No Consciousness (Dreamless Sleep)	O C	A	Full Consciousness

Illustration 4.1

In illustration 4.1, OC is the window of consciousness. The larger the window, the more aware we are of ourselves and our surroundings, and vice versa. The point C keeps moving on the axis. If the point lies exactly over O, it is a state of complete unconsciousness. If it lies over A, it is a state of full consciousness.

Within the consciousness window, there is a hierarchy of sensations we may be conscious about. If we are watching a movie on TV, we will be more conscious about the movie than the TV stand, and even less conscious about the carpet in the room even though they all fall within our consciousness window. Thus, consciousness window can also be imagined as a circle in which level of consciousness fades away, as we move from the centre of the circle of the circle toward the circumference. What lies outside falls under our subconscious mind.

According to IPA, there are three modes of consciousness:

1. Alpha Consciousness: When input information is getting processed by both low-level and high-level processors. Here, we look at the present based on our past conditioning (of high-level processors). It is the kind of consciousness we experience in our daily lives.

2. Beta Consciousness: Here, the information is processed only by low-level processors and high-level processors process information only voluntarily, if not at all. Here, we look at the

Time: Unreal, Unstable, Unreliable?

Time is an illusion.

—*Albert Einstein*

What is time? We generally relate time with the time shown by our watches and phones. This standard time helps us in interacting and coordinating with others. But time is not as uniform and standard as commonly understood and felt.

The concept of time is closely related to that of consciousness. Here, time refers to psychological time and not to the external time as shown by a clock. We have an inherent sense of time. When we wait for someone, time seems to move very slowly, whereas if we are watching a gripping movie, time seems to move very fast. Here, wherever the term 'time' is used, it refers to psychological time.

First, let us lay out the hypothesis regarding time, and then see if it matches with our observations.

The hypothesis: *the larger the window of consciousness, slower becomes time, and vice versa.*

Here, what do we mean by 'slower'? It means slower compared to external time.

Let us take the extreme case first. In the state of dreamless sleep, the size of consciousness window is zero. Here, psychological time moves at a very fast speed compared to the external time. Suppose you go to sleep at 11 p.m. and wake up at 6 a.m. the next morning without any intervening dreams. If you had a sound sleep, you would feel only a split second has passed between your sleeping and waking up. For you, the psychological passage of time is less than one second, almost zero, whereas the external time has moved by seven hours. Thus, the rate of change of external time (seconds) is:

$$\frac{Change\ in\ external\ time}{Change\ in\ psychological\ time} = \frac{7X60X60}{0} \approx Infinite$$

As the window of consciousness starts expanding, psychological time seems to move closely with the external time. There might be a scenario when your psychological time is moving exactly at the speed of external time. In this case, the rate of change of external time would be one. Your internal clock would be exactly matched with the external one.

As the window of consciousness expands even further, external time seems to go even slower. In fact, in the state of full consciousness, the rate of change of external time approaches zero. One nanosecond of external time might seem like hours of psychological time. Eventually, time ceases to exist. One would feel completely absorbed in the present. Thus, with some oversimplification, the rate of change of external time in this case is (only an example for understanding):

$$\frac{Change\ in\ external\ time}{Change\ in\ psychological\ time} = \frac{Nanosecond}{Hours} \approx 0$$

From IPA's perspective, it makes perfect sense. When we are in dreamless sleep, only low-level processors are active. When we wake up, first, the older high-level processors become active (when we open our eyes after waking up, things seem blurry as we see things in rudimentary fashion). But as our consciousness window expands during the course of day, the newer processors (on chronological scale) might come into action. As we would approach pure consciousness, processing shifts from old high-level processors to new high-level processors. When we become fully conscious, time would seize to exist. It may not seem intuitive at all, but it is the logical coherent extreme end of the spectrum.

Breathing: Elixir of Life

Feelings come and go like clouds in a windy sky. Conscious breathing is my anchor.

—*Thich Nhat Hanh*

Breathing is what gives life to us. It is fundamental to the principle of life, and yet we take it for granted. Sometimes, even days pass without realizing consciously that we are breathing. Yet, if understood properly, it can have profound impact on the way we live our lives.

Breathing is closely related to consciousness and time. It is an outwardly manifestation of the state of consciousness at a point in time. Just as the handwriting of a person can reveal about a person's personality traits, the pattern of breathing can tell us about a person's state of consciousness and mind.

Let us find out how it is related to consciousness. If the size of window of consciousness is not steady, it would result in uneven breathing. Thus, if we observe our breath closely and find it to be uneven, it is an indication that our consciousness window is unstable. This could happen if one or more thoughts have taken over our mind, and their energy demand is such that the pattern of breathing is altered. In the figure depicting the consciousness window, imagine the point C moving erratically left and right on the axis. When we are experiencing negative emotions like fear, anxiety, depression, our breathing pattern becomes very uneven, and it is physiologically not very healthy. Therefore, if a person experiencing such emotions consciously alters his breathing pattern and tries to make it more even, it can help in overcoming those feelings, but he will feel a lot resistance from the mind. The ensuing negative thought would try its best to not get dethroned from the mind.

Uniform breathing would indicate a stable window of consciousness. Longer the time it is stable for, its size would keep increasing. Therefore, most of the meditation techniques involve regulation of breath. The more uniform the breathing pattern is, the larger and more stable would be the window of consciousness. It is a way to train the mind to be calm and energy efficient (the more unstable it is, more energy is being used by it).

A natural corollary of this is the sensation of time. The slower we breathe, the slower seems the psychological time, and vice versa. Slower the psychological time, we are more in the present moment. This is also an objective of most meditation techniques (i.e., to stay in the present). The longer the meditation session, the slower the psychological time would be the person would feel more relaxed and peaceful.

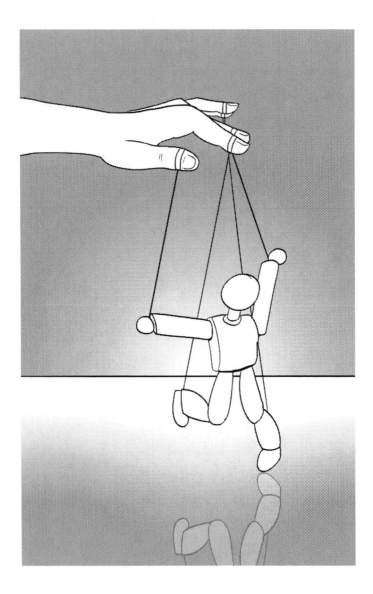

Free Will: Relax, It's Not You

Man can do what he wills, but he cannot will what he wills.

—Arthur Schopenhauer

Do we have the power to choose? Have you felt you have no control whatsoever over your decisions? Before going further, I must emphasize that the quest for truth should be with an open mind. One should at least give a chance to understand it no matter how counterintuitive and inconvenient it may sound.

We have tried to understand consciousness and 'I' from Information Processing Approach. We have understood how there is no permanent entity as 'self.' We have also understood how the thought processors of similar input information range and quality create an illusion that there is a permanent entity 'I,' which chooses one of the two or more possible scenarios based on the outputs generated by the processors.

Thus, the next logical question is if there is no permanent 'I,' about whose free will are we talking about? In colloquial terms, free will would mean if you have choice A and choice B, you can choose either.

But as we have seen, our choice is not determined by a permanent 'I,' but rather by the comparative strength of competing processors. When the input sensation is getting processed by one of the processors, we become that processor and that gives a sensation of 'I,' which is temporary. Then we become the other processor, and finally after deliberations, the output is generated by one of the processors giving an illusion that we have made a choice.

According to Malcolm Gladwell in his book *Blink: The Power of Thinking Without Thinking* [research] suggests that what we think of as free will is largely an illusion. Much of the time, we are simply operating on automatic pilot and the way we think and act, how well we think and act on the spur of the moment are a lot more susceptible to outside influences than we realize. This does not necessarily mean that things are deterministic. In a particular situation for an input information, which of the competing processors win, would depend on the state of mind. Therefore, it cannot be conclusively established beforehand which input sensation will eventually be processed by which processor.

Here, the physical nature of thought processors (corresponding physical manifestation of a processor) would play a key role. If they are 'large' in size, they will be governed by Newtonian physics and would point toward complete determinism. If they are very small particles governed by quantum principles, it might leave a scope for free will, but not of the kind we normally envisage.

But what would happen if we are in the mode of beta consciousness? The processors above stage 3 would become inactive. If the mind would receive input information beyond stage 3, it will not be processed at all. The chain of input-process-output-input will be stopped there itself. There will be no chain of cause-effect. Will this be considered as free will? We will not be determined in our thought and action by the input information. We will be completely present, and will merely react to external stimuli without any conditioning. We will be free of the cause-effect cycle. We will discuss more about free will in the second part of the book.

Expectations: Ever Bullish

Blessed is he who expects nothing for he shall never be disappointed.

—Alexander Pope

When we drop a tennis ball on the floor, we expect it to bounce back. Why do we do so? Knowing the Newton's laws of motion, we know why the ball comes up and thus we expect it to do so. But knowing the laws of motion is not the reason why we expect the ball to come back up. Even before Newton was born, people would have expected a rubber ball to come up when thrown toward the ground.

Thus, while the phenomena of a ball bouncing back can be very accurately explained by laws of physics, we do not need the knowledge of such a law to expect it to happen. We expect it to happen because we have seen it happening several times in the past, and before us, our ancestors and their ancestors have experienced it.

But let's say, when you throw the ball on the floor tomorrow, it does not come back. You will obviously be surprised. The exact reason for the surprise will not be that the ball didn't conform to the laws of physics.

Rather, the real reason will be that you did not expect it to not come back.

The more number of times you have seen it happening, the stronger your expectation would be for the result. Obviously, knowing the laws of physics would further reinforce it.

From IPA perspective, this expectation is the result of the processing of input information taking place in the processors. The older the processors, the stronger would be the expectation of the future course of event. (Processor -> Conditioning -> Expectation)

Expectations can be put in three categories:

i. *Expectation from the physical world*: We expect the ball to bounce back. We expect plants to grow. Based on such expectations, we make sense of the world.

ii. *Expectation from people around us*: We have different levels of expectations from different people. We cannot expect from a stranger what we may expect from a family member.

iii. *Expectation from ourselves*: Based on our thoughts and actions from the past, we expect ourselves to think and act in a particular way in a situation.

What happens when the events don't take place as expected?

As we have seen before, expectation is a manifestation of outputs yielded by information processors, which are formed by repetition of occurrences (or producing the same output for an input every time). The deviation of actual event from the expected course alters a particular processor. If the deviation is repeated many times, the corresponding processor also undergoes change or a new processor might even get formed. But if the processor is too rigid and inelastic, it might resist change dissipating a lot of energy.

From this, we can draw an important inference. Suppose we are expecting an event A to occur, which is associated with pleasure. But the actual event A is different from A. The magnitude and direction of deviation would determine what would happen next.

i. If it gives more pleasure than expected, the corresponding processor would take considerably lesser energy to change. The next time similar input is received by that processor (high-level processor), it would give an output (thought) expecting more pleasure than before.

ii. If the deviation is on the side of lesser than expected pleasure (or even pain), the processor would resist a structural change as pain or 'less pleasure' will be resisted by the mind. Thus, more energy would be spent in making even a small change in the processor. Next time, if the processor receives a similar input, its output (thought) would indicate less pleasure than the previous case, but its magnitude would be lower compared to the first scenario.

Thus, what we have understood here is that processors themselves can change. If we experience more pleasure than expected, then from the next time our expectation is readjusted in the direction of more pleasure. If we experience less pleasure than expected, then from the next time our expectation is readjusted in the direction of less pleasure. The quantum of readjustment is much higher in the former than the latter.

For example, if you are expecting a 10 per cent salary hike from your company, but you get a 15 per cent hike, you will derive a lot of pleasure; but next time you might expect a 20 per cent hike. Even if you get a 20 per cent hike, you might not be as happy as the previous time even though the salary has increased by five percent in both the cases.

But suppose you were expecting a 15 per cent hike, instead, you get a 12 per cent hike—the relative sadness would be same if not more than the relative happiness you felt when your hike exceeded your expectations. But you would not readjust your expectation to 9 per cent; rather, your expectation is likely to stay at 15 per cent if not more.

This is commonly referred to as negativity bias.

Happiness: Ever Bearish

*Man is fond of counting his troubles,
but he does not count his joys. If he counted
them up as he ought to, he would see that
every lot has enough happiness provided
for it.*

—Fyodor Dostoevsky

What is happiness? It is probably the most sought after thing by us, and yet it is so elusive. Happiness means different things to different people. A poor person might be happy if he gets all his meals, a mother might be happy if her children do well, a cancer patient might become happy if he comes to know that he can be cured, and a rich person might be happy to buy the latest model of his favourite car brand. Every person needs food, clothing, and shelter to survive. But beyond this happiness is a relative idea. A common theme behind different ideas of happiness is the presence of pleasure and absence of pain (physical and mental). Evolutionarily, we are programmed to maximize pleasure and minimize pain. Even if someone gets happiness by doing charity, he is also driven by the mental pleasure he derives by helping others.

If happiness is considered as presence of pleasure and absence of pain, then lasting happiness is very difficult to achieve because when you attain a particular pleasure, the happiness derived from it will gradually diminish as expectations (or processors) would readjust according to the new scenario (as discussed in the previous section).Now, for being happy, you must find a new source of pleasure, which would again be short-lived and every next time it would become even harder to find a source of happiness because the expectation would have readjusted to an even higher value. But yet, we have a conception that happiness is a fixed entity, which we can chase and get. In 1978, a research conducted by researchers from Northwestern University and University of Massachusetts suggested that people who won jackpot lotteries were actually less happy after some time than before winning the lottery. This is a perfect example of how fulfilment of high expectations actually makes it difficult to sustain happiness.

So what then is 'true sustainable happiness'? From the IPA perspective, true happiness would be when the expectations (or processors) don't readjust automatically. But as long as they would process information, they would readjust. That is how we are programmed. Therefore, *not expecting* anything might lead to true happiness. But is it even possible? Expectation is derived from the past, from our memory, and our conditioning. It is the basis on which our lives are lived. But if we can manage to stay completely in the present, that is in every moment as it passes by that could be the state of happiness devoid of any expectations and thus sustainable. Here, a parallel with the phrase from the Bhagavad Gita, Nishkam Karma, can be drawn. Krishna asks Arjuna to work without expecting any results.

An idea related to how the mind works vis-à-vis expectations is *Negativity Bias*. It has been a popular idea for quite some time. It means we get disproportionately affected by pain than by pleasure. This can be easily understood as a corollary of explanation of expectations in the previous section. Negativity bias can explain why most people are dissatisfied with their lives even if they have what they apparently need for a happy life. We will use the idea of negativity bias to understand job satisfaction later in the book.

Knowing: Order of Ignorance

*I am the wisest man alive, for I know one
thing, and that is that I know nothing.*

—Plato

What does it mean to know something? It is easy to say
that you know your name or you know a week has seven
days. But do you know that you should save water, as it is
a scarce commodity? If you know, do you do it sincerely?
If you don't, what is the reason behind? An obese person
knows he must not eat food with high calories, but still
cannot prevent himself from having his favourite sweets.
So when do we truly know something? IPA can help us
answer that question.

'Knowing' has many levels; the different levels of
knowing create corresponding gaps between knowing
and doing. When I prick a pin in your arm, you know
very well that it hurts you immediately react. There is no
lag between knowing and doing. This is because there
is no confusion for the input information as to which
processor it has to go through. There is a unique output
possible for the input and the processing is lightning
fast (low-level processor). No other processor can even
remotely process this input.

But when we move above this stage (i.e., at the thought level), there is no definite output for an input information. Two or more processors are capable of handling information of similar range and quality. Depending on the state of mind, one of the processors would win.

If over a period of time one processor keeps winning over another, the relation between input and output would start becoming one to one. This would feel like we know the fact. For example, if we want to switch on a light bulb, we know that a switch must be turned on. This has been reinforced over the years, and thus there is no doubt about what would lead to switching on of a light bulb. In fact, it happens with most of us that when we enter a familiar room—say our bedroom or study room—our hands automatically move toward the switchboard to switch the light on, sometimes without even consciously thinking about it.

But there will be a distinction between knowing something at the thought level or intellectual level, and knowing something at the level of lower processors or the experiential level.

As we have seen, low-level processors have been formed over millions of years, and thus when information is processed by them, the accompanying chemical reaction causing physiological changes is quick and potent. In the case of thought-level processors, the potency of accompanying chemical reaction is low, and thus the physiological changes are also of milder nature.

Let's take an example to emphasize the point. It is one thing to know (at intellectual level) that we should not handle electric switches with wet hands when told by someone, and it is another thing to know it (at experiential level) after getting an electric shock while doing so.

This difference in levels of knowing often creates dissonance in our minds. If we know something merely at the intellectual level, and not at the experiential level, we might be pulled into different directions as the knowledge would not have percolated from thought-level processors to low-level processors.

Conflict: Tug of War

A man's own self is his friend. A man's own self is his foe.

—Bhagvad Gita

All of us experience conflict at some level. There are conflicts in our families, in our professional lives, and within us. Can IPA help us in understanding conflicts? Let us try to understand conflicts within ourselves.

Till the lower stages of input processors, there is one to one relation between input information and information processor (i.e., input information can be processed by only one processor).

But at higher stages, input information can be processed by more than one processor depending on the quality and range of information. Whenever a processor processes information, there takes place an accompanying chemical reaction bringing about physiological change of varying degrees sometimes visible and sometimes not visible.

What would happen if two processors process the same input information causing chemical reactions resulting in physiological changes, which oppose each other? For example, you see a chocolate cake on the table. After passing through the low-level processors, the input information (after modifications) reaches thought-level processors. When processed by first processor, chemicals are secreted, which give a sensation that you want to eat the cake, as it is very tempting.

Simultaneously, when passed through the second processor, the accompanying sensation is that of not eating the cake as it has a lot of calories. Thus, your mind is giving contradictory orders to your body. But what you do ultimately depends on which processor wins the competition and ultimately releases the chemicals, which actually make you eat or not eat the cake.

Here, there is a distinction between the thought of eating the cake and actually eating the cake. Here, the initial battle was between the thought processors. These processors didn't produce chemicals, which gave us a semblance of sensation of the two scenarios based on past experience. The actual behaviour takes place when the chemicals produced are potent enough to produce a strong and visible psychological change.

If such mental conflicts continue in the mind for a long time, that would result in a lot of energy dissipation leading to lethargy causing a sensation of feeling low.

The energy loss is on account of the two factors. Firstly, there is a constant switching of 'I' between the two states (i.e., 'I' want to eat cake and 'I' should not eat cake). Secondly, it is on account of the contradictory nature of physiological changes being produced in the body.

If there was only one processor through which the input information could have passed based on its quality and range, there would not have been any conflict. Mental conflicts can be resolved using meditation. I have described a specific method to get instant relief from conflict in the third part of the book.

Fear: Friend or Nemesis

Nothing in life is to be feared, it is only to be understood. Now is the time to understand more, so that we may fear less.

—Marie Curie

We have identified 'pleasure-pain' as one of the low-level processors. It has been so instrumental in the survival of our species during evolution that it is hardwired into us (thus, a low-level processor).

Had there been a species, which did not feel pain, it would not have survived. Pain is the first level of defence for survival. We try to avoid pain as much as possible.

Similarly, had a species not experienced pleasure, it would not have survived. After all, mating takes place between two organisms of a species, and is driven by the sense of pleasure. Therefore, we wish to attain as much pleasure as possible. As already discussed, high-level processors are derivatives of low-level processors, and thus carry their characteristics. Thus, along with the physical level, at the mental level also, we try to avoid pain and attain pleasure.

Here, we need to draw the distinction between physical and psychological pleasure and pain. The pain or pleasure sensation generated directly by the low-level processors can be called physical and sensations generated by high-level processors can be called psychological.

Now, what then is fear? Fear is a reactionary feeling when we encounter an input, which is representative of an imminent situation, which would increase pain or reduce pleasure—be it real or imagined. If we see a snake on the ground, we are afraid and react immediately by either moving away immediately or by attacking it. This is physical fear.

But sometimes, we get afraid merely by the thought of a snake when in fact there is no snake around. This is psychological fear. While physical fear is caused by processing of low-level of processors, psychological fear is caused by high-level processors (which are further derivatives of low-level processors). The feeling of fear, no matter of what it is, has some common quality indicating a unifying characteristic in different kinds of fear.

While physical fear works at a very fundamental level, and broadly speaking, is a reality of life, psychological fear works differently. It can be experienced only through thoughts (and thought coming from high-level processors have the characteristics of low-level processors including the pleasure-pain processor). So if you are not having thoughts in your mind, there cannot be any psychological fear. As discussed before, as thoughts create a sensation of self, that self by default tries to avoid pain and attaches to pleasure. Thus, it is accompanied by fear of pain or fear of loss of pleasure.

Next time when you experience a fearful thought, try to observe that thought closely. You will see that that very thought is the thinker itself (of that thought). There is no separate self that experiences the thought; rather, it is the thought that experiences itself. If you can realize this at that moment, the fear would dissolve.

Thought is ephemeral in nature. But when it arises, it tries to seek permanence by hijacking the mind and becoming the self. This leads us to believe that we are the thinkers of the thoughts, but actually, it is the thought, which thinks itself. We buy this illusion and get entangled in the content of the thought. For example, most of us fear about what will happen in the future whether we would be healthy, successful, and recognized. Here, instead of trying to come to a conclusive answer, which is almost impossible if we can observe the process of occurrence of thought itself, the thought along with the fear would dissolve. This is not easy and comes only through practice.

Anxiety is the feeling when we perceive that an anticipated fear has a high probability of coming true. Thus, anxiety is always associated with fear. There is hardly any anxiety with physical fear because we immediately react to avoid or deal with it. If we see a snake, we immediately act. There is no time for anxiety.

In the case of psychological fear, however, the event associated with fear may not happen immediately or may not happen at all. But if the mind perceives that it is almost certain to happen, it causes anxiety.

From IPA's perspective, when we experience psychological fear, it is accompanied by a change, which acts as input information for another processor. When processed by this processor, another change is produced, which gives a sensation of anxiety. This change consumes a lot of energy making a person feel low and depressed.

As anxiety is associated with fear, so it can also be dealt by understanding the reason behind its cause, which is also a thought. The traditional way of dealing with anxiety is to try to change the external factors that cause anxiety. But it can be better dealt with if we can observe the thought behind the anxiety. This is very difficult especially because when someone is anxious, it feels as if one is caught in a storm. The more one tries to get rid of it, the stronger the storm becomes. But with better understanding and practice, one can see anxiety getting dissolved in the calmness of mind. In the last chapter of the book, I have discussed some meditation techniques that can help us in such situations.

Boredom: Underrated

Is life not a thousand times too short
for us to bore ourselves?

—Friedrich Nietzsche

Boredom has become a very common phenomenon. We are surrounded by so many avenues of engagement, and yet we so easily get bored. The ordeal of boredom can be very painful and I believe it is underrated. It is a very real problem.

Understanding boredom from the perspective of IPA is very interesting. In common parlance, boredom is understood as lack of engagement with external (people, action, etc.) or the internal (thoughts, feelings, etc.). From IPA's perspective, it refers to a mental state when most of the processors are not receiving any input information, and thus there is no accompanying change.

But why do we try to escape boredom? There is a discomfort which we feel—it could be anxiety, depression, etc.—which prompts us to look for an engaging activity or thought; for example, watching TV, reading a book, and most commonly, using our smart phones.

Before we try to understand the reason behind this discomfort, let's try to juxtapose the feeling of boredom with the feeling experienced just after meditation. In this state also, we are not engaged with any activity or thought, and yet we are not uncomfortable about the situation. For convenience sake, if we describe the post meditation feeling as blissful, then there is a lot of similarity between feelings of boredom and bliss. In both situations, we do not actively engage with a thought or activity.

But there is a significant difference between the two states of mind. Let us apply principles of IPA to both the situations and understand the difference.

As discussed before, processors are formed as a result of repeated habits. These processors require certain energy to operate, which they draw from the mind based on past history. Imagine, a person who has been working in a job for thirty years stops going to office. When he used to go to office, there were certain activities he used to perform like working on files, talking to colleagues, etc. The processor involved in these activities must have been reinforced over the years, and draw certain energy for processing these activities. Now suddenly, they stop receiving any input information. This leaves some residual unused energy with the processors. If this energy is not diverted to other processors to perform certain activities, there is a surplus. Following situations may arise:

i. The processors which can utilize this energy can pick input information from the internal interface or memory and start processing them

    a. If these processors have a heavy component of pain meta-processors, feelings like fear and anxiety would be produced

    b. If these processors have a heavy component of pleasure, feelings like happiness and elation would be produced

ii. If no processors are able to get input information, it would be understood by the mind as its functioning is not required, as no input information of expected quality and range is being received. Basically, the mind would take it as signal to go into a low energy or sleep mode. As a result, the mind would secrete chemicals, which would lower the energy available to the processors giving a sensation of feeling low or sleepy. Thus, mind starts functioning at a low energy state.

But if one or more processors start receiving input information, which require relatively high energy, then the mind switches to a high-energy mode. For example, a person is alone and feeling bored and gets a call from his old school friend. This input information gets processed by certain processors, which require relatively higher energy, which is allocated by the mind. This is a signal to the mind to switch to high-energy mode.

In the case of blissful feeling, what happens is that the subject is not engaged in a thought or activity. But here, instead of some latent processors getting activated (situation 1) or the mind going to low energy mode (situation 2), the mind continues to stay in high-energy mode and the processors also remain inactive. The relation between the two states can be understood through an analogy. At zero degrees Celsius, water can exist as both liquid and ice. But to convert ice into water, latent heat is required. Similarly, for making a switch from the state of boredom to bliss, focused energy is required.

It is possible to make a switch from the state of boredom to the state of calm bliss if one has control over their minds. Focusing on an object or breath for some time can pull the mind from the state of low energy to high energy. Another way to get rid of boredom is to divert the mind to some other engaging activity, but this would not lead to a blissful state. Physical exercise is also a useful way of increasing the energy level of mind.

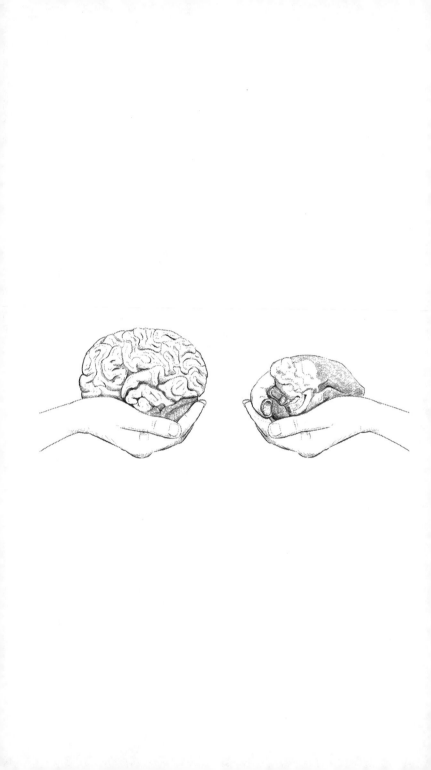

Pledger Account: Logical Versus Emotional

> Emotions have taught mankind to reason.
>
> —Marquis De Vauvenargues

We often use the words logic and emotion. They are particularly seen as means to arriving at an act. They are often treated as two different approaches of arriving at a decision, and are commonly assumed to be contrary to each other. Here, however, I would like to argue that these are not contrary to each other.

These two words—logic and emotion—are mental constructs, and it is difficult to find a universally agreed upon definition for them. How can we use IPA to understand and distinguish between them? We have learnt about meta-processors. One of them, the pain-pleasure meta-processor, plays a key role in deciding whether an act is perceived as logical or emotional.

What is it to be logical? Here, we are deliberately focusing on the person and not the act itself. For example, we will not be arguing whether 2+2=4 is logical or not. Let us take another example. There is delicious chocolate cake lying in front of you. Would you eat it? If there are no other factors involved, like your concern for calorie count or the hygiene factor, you would eat the cake as it will increase your pleasure. Thus, we can say it is logical that you eat the cake. But what if more variables are introduced (e.g., you are a diabetic patient or you are dieting). Now, it is not logical to eat the cake because it can potentially increase your pain in the long run. To make things clear, let us assume a variable P, which is the difference between the perceived pleasure and pain (mind quantifies them roughly and tacitly) derived by performing an act.

Thus, for a particular action and a particular person, P can be defined as:

$$P = \text{Perceived pleasure} - \text{Perceived pain}$$

If P is positive, the person would feel he is logical; else, he is illogical. Here, I would like to lay emphasis on the need to understand an act from different perspectives. For the person performing the act, P will be always positive when calculated at that very moment of time. Later on, he might calculate a different value of P for the same action. Thus, from the reference frame of the person who performed the action, P is always positive; and thus, he is always logical while performing the act. It is only later that he might perceive the value of P differently. Also, an external observer might calculate P very differently from the person who performed the act. At this point, I would urge you to refrain from mixing this with the colloquial meaning of logic, and I will be discussing emotion separately soon.

Now let's take an example. A terrorist agrees to become a suicide bomber. You might ask how on earth is that logical from his perspective. It is logical from his perspective because he has been made to believe that either it is the right thing to do (and he derives great pleasure by doing the right thing), or he has been made to believe that he will have a lot of pleasure after death (maybe because he would go to heaven or because his family would be taken care of). As a result, for him, the net value of P is positive. It might seem completely illogical from the perspective of an external observer, and even by the terrorist himself after some time (only if he survives).

Another example would make things clearer. You want to lose weight, and for that, you start running two miles every morning. You are not a morning person, but you still endeavour to wake up at 5 a.m. every day. This part is very painful, but at the subconscious level, you have calculated that the pleasure derived by losing the weight would more than compensate for the pain caused by running every day. Hence P would be positive. Thus, it becomes logical for you.

On some days, when you wake up, the mind would give you arguments as to why it is not worth waking up so early and you should rather go back to sleep. At that particular moment, the value of pleasure derived by sleeping an extra ten minutes might seem very high and push you to hit the snooze button. In case you do hit the snooze button a few times and eventually skip your running for the day, you will have a feeling of guilt later that day. We will talk about guilt shortly.

It also depends how others view your pain and pleasure dynamics. If they feel that you are already very thin, then for them, it would be illogical for you to make so much effort. The concept of pain and pleasure itself can be subjective, especially at subtle levels. It would also depend on the belief system of a society you live in. It could be possible in a certain society people derive a lot of pleasure by waking up early in the morning to see the sunrise. For them, not waking up in the morning could be lowering of pleasure.

Everyone inherently tries to maximize the value of their P. There are three ways of doing that in the context of pain-pleasure dynamics:

i)   Maximizing pleasure

ii) Minimizing pain

iii) Both the above together

The type of people who are more concerned with maximizing pleasure even if it could lead to more pain are more likely to take risks in their lives and decisions, whereas the second category of people are less prone to taking risks as they want to avoid pain at any cost.

Guilt

Going back to the 'waking early in the morning' example, why does the person feel guilty if he didn't wake up on time? Let us understand from where does guilt come from. Guilt is always associated with hindsight. As I said before, at the moment of doing an act, the act seems logical to the doer as the value of P is positive. But in the future, it is possible that the person again calculates P for the same act, and it comes out to be negative or less than the value calculated before. This could give a sensation of guilt to the person. Larger the difference, more would be the guilt. Guilt might also be accompanied by anger. But it may not be the same across all people. For some, a small value of difference in P could cause more guilt and vice versa.

Also, people who derive a lot of pleasure by doing the right thing are more prone to feeling guilty. They always want to be right because of the pleasure they derive from it (consciously or subconsciously). This want makes them calculate P for an act again and again at different points in time. This makes it more likely that a lower value of P (compared to the original one) would be calculated by them at some point. Every time they calculate a lower value of P, they feel guilty. I would reiterate here that this calculation takes place most of the times subconsciously.

People might have very different ways of deriving pleasure and minimizing pain. For some people, the highest form of pleasure might be doing the right thing. This right thing would depend on his belief systems, which would be heavily influenced by the belief system of family and society. For some, physical pleasure might be the highest form of pleasure. Some people might derive pleasure by being recognized by others. They might do stuff that gives them pain, but in return give recognition and acceptance by the society (e.g., tattoo or nose piercing). Similarly, people might have different ways of minimizing pain. Some people can go to the extent of killing themselves to minimize pain. This shows there is so much subjectivity in the matters of pain and pleasure.

Thus, a logical act is one where the value of P calculated by the doer for that act is positive. But there is an interesting twist to it. In the calculation of P, pain and pleasure values are adjusted for future returns also. For example, avoiding the temptation to eat a high calorie cake might be painful at that moment, but in the long run, the pleasure derived would make the value P positive. Similarly, taking the pain to wake up early in the morning for running is an investment to draw more pleasure in the future. It is like depositing an amount in the bank to receive interests some time later. It is a case of postponed increase of pleasure or decrease of pain.

Thus, we can say a person seems logical with respect to an act if the value of P is positive (either calculated by him or someone else). Now, what do we mean by illogical? Let us take an example to understand this. You eat a cake even if you are a diabetic (and have been advised against it by the doctor). This is an illogical action because it can increase your pain in future. But it is illogical from the perspective of another person or from the perspective of a 'future you.' When you ate the cake, the value of

P for you was positive, and thus the act was logical at that time. Such illogical acts are colloquially recognized and called as acts driven by emotion. Generally, a very emotional person is perceived as foolish because his acts are different from the accepted norms (positive P). There is no qualitative difference as such between logical and emotional decisions. In fact, for the doer, every action is logical. For the perceiver, it may seem logical or emotional based on his calculation of P.

We often talk about the confusion and conflict between head and heart or logic and emotion. Here, the conflict is actually within the person. He is calculating P from two reference points and not getting a conclusive answer as to which course would have higher P.

So what does one do when caught between the pulls of logic and emotion before making a decision? One must first understand that logic and emotion are not two different sources of voices reaching their heads, one from the head and other from the heart (figuratively speaking); rather, both the voices are coming from the same place. The person is confused mainly because the value of P calculated in both the cases (logic and emotion) are either in isolation unclear (lies over a wide range) or pretty close to each other. Thus, the mind is not able to conclusively decide the course of action.

This is why it is often said when a person is confused before making a decision, he should set his priorities right. Setting priorities right means assigning a concrete score to different variables based on the person's perceptions. If the scores are clearly assigned to the variables based on the pain-pleasure principle, the calculation of P automatically becomes easy and clear. Once the values of P in different scenarios become clear, it becomes easier to arrive at a decision. That decision is always logical from the doer's point of view at that very moment. The doer might see the values of P differently later on, and feel he could have done things differently. Other people might observe the action as logical or emotional based on their perception of the value of P.

Different people have different abilities of calculating the value of P for different situations depending on their physiology, external environment, and past conditioning. Some people are naturally good at calculating the value of P. They can easily assign values based on pain-pleasure dynamics to different actions (their priorities are straight). Their processors are stronger, and there is less ambiguity as to a particular information would be processed by which processor. Thus, they are perceived as people who are sure of themselves. For some people, it does not come naturally to assign accurate scores to different courses of actions and decision making becomes difficult for them. They may feel confused very often, and could also be perceived as confused by others.

Normally, emotional intelligence is defined as 'the capacity of individuals to recognize their own and other people's emotions to discriminate between different feelings and label them appropriately, and to use emotional information to guide thinking and behaviour' (Wikipedia). I think the definition should also include (explicitly) one's ability to prioritize or assign values to different courses of action based on the pain-pleasure dynamics.

Utilitarianism

The theory of utilitarianism is based on the balance of pleasure over pain. It is applied at the level of an individual, society, or country to determine what is the right thing to do. It is based on the rule of 'Greatest Happiness for The Greatest Number.' If an act results in the increase of overall happiness of a society, it is perceived as the right thing to do and vice versa. Happiness is derived by maximizing pleasure and minimizing pain. But the practical problem faced here is the calculation of perceived happiness because there is no standard barometer of happiness. Firstly, people derive happiness from their own value of P and thus there is no uniformity in the idea of happiness. For example, a person might be very happy simply by watching TV the whole day, but another person might get very bored doing so and would be happier to do some outdoor activity. Secondly, it is impossible to accurately measure someone's happiness. We have to rely on people's own perception, which makes it very subjective and difficult to measure.

Faith and Logic

It will be interesting to introduce the word faith in our discussions at this point. What is faith? How is it different from logic? We have discussed how a person decides to act in a certain way based on the value of P (perceived pleasure–perceived pain) calculated by him consciously or subconsciously. The value of perceived pleasure and pain is further dependent on other variables making the calculation complex sometimes. If the number of variables is less and their values do not seem vague, we intuitively understand how a particular value of P is arrived at. In such a scenario, the act seems to be done clearly based on logic. For example, if you are hungry, you will eat food. Here, the variables involved in the calculation of P are simple. We can very clearly see why this act would give more pleasure than pain (i.e., the value of P is positive). Thus, it seems quite logical to eat food when hungry. But in situations where the calculation of P becomes complicated because of the nature of variables involved in that situation, and difficulty in assigning them clear values it would seem the act has been performed out of faith rather than logic.

For example, a lot of people who want to become entrepreneurs have to take a call at some point to take risk by quitting their jobs. Here, the dynamics of arriving at a value of P are very complex and vague. Still, they take a decision, say by quitting their jobs, based on a positive value of P. But the steps in the calculation of this value are not very clear to that person because there are too many variables, and it is difficult to assign accurate values to them. Thus, it seems that the decision has been made more on the basis of faith than logic.

Here, there is no qualitative difference between logic and faith. The principle behind decision making remains the same. It is simply the complexity of calculation, which makes it seem based either on logic or faith. Taking it one step further, we can also ask ourselves whether logic is itself based on faith. As the complexity of calculation of P behind a logical decision is relatively simpler, it gives a comfort of certainty that the P calculated at a different time would give a similar result. But there is no absolute certainty here. Rather, there is a high probability. For decisions based on faith, because of the complexity in the calculation of P, there is low probability that the value of P will be similar when calculated at different times. It is a matter of probability whether high or low. Thus, we can say, we take a leap of faith even when we are making logical decisions. It is just that we have more faith in logic.

Echoing Sentiments:
Parallels with Other Philosophies

There is no God higher than truth.

—Mahatma Gandhi

Up till now in the journey through the book, we have developed the idea of how the human mind acts as an information processor and have evaluated the various mental states associated with fear, anxiety, boredom, etc. through the lens of IPA. Such mental states have been associated with the idea of human suffering in traditional philosophies and religions. Let us explore some of them further.

1) Buddhism

According to Buddhism, ignorance is the root cause of suffering. Pratityasamitpada is the theory of causation in Buddhism according to which effect exists as long as its cause exists. Based on this, the concept of Dharma Chakra is given. According to Buddha, we are caught in a long chain of cause and effect, which is responsible for our sufferings. To get rid of sufferings, we must get out of this chain. We can get out of the chain if we can overcome ignorance, which is one of the links in the chain.

This can also be understood from the perspective of Information Processing Approach. We have seen how thoughts, feelings, and actions are determined by low-level and high-level processors. If we see closely, this is also like a cause and effect chain where input information is the cause and change yielded by processor is the effect. If the processors become inactive and the incessant flow of processing and output of information ceases, we will become free from this cycle of input and output over which we have no control.

2) Bhagavad Gita

One of the most important messages of Bhagavad Gita is based on the theory of karma. Good deeds contribute to good karma and future happiness, and bad deeds contribute to bad karma and future suffering. As long as we are in the karmic cycle, we will be in bondage. Getting out of the cycle will lead to liberation, which is called Moksha.

From IPA perspective, it means that as long as information is getting processed by the high-level processors, we don't have any free will whatsoever, and we are helplessly governed by the input information and their processing. But as soon as the high-level processors would stop processing information, we would become free.

In the Bhagavad Gita, the path toward Moksha is through 'Nishkam Karma' or working without any desire toward the result. Expecting a result is one of the key characteristics of high-level or thought processors (as processors themselves are a result of past habits and experiences). If we are fully conscious (i.e., high-level processors become inactive), we will look at things without any conditioning. If we look at things without conditioning, we would not expect events to take a particular course. We will be completely immersed in the present moment, and that, according to Bhagavad Gita, would be the state of liberation.

PART II:

The Universe, God, Love, and Morality

Underneath this reality in which we live and have our being, another and altogether different reality lies concealed.

—Friedrich Nietzsche

Nature of Universe:
Press Start to Begin

If you wish to make an apple pie from scratch, you must first invent the universe.'

'We are a way for the cosmos to know itself.

—*Carl Sagan*

Till now, we have tried to understand how our mind works based on Information Processing Approach. Now, I would argue that it is not just the mind or the body, but everything in the universe including inanimate things can be governed by information processing. As the processors in living beings process information and cause change, non-living things also process information, and changes occur if the input information corresponds to quality and range handled by a particular processor. The difference between living beings and non-living things lie in the complexity of processors. The processors of living beings are capable of processing a wide quality of information, and a subtle change in the input information might result in a drastically different 'change.'

For example, a wooden four-legged table is encoded in a certain way. It has a rudimentary processor and can process information of a particular quality. If I throw a hammer on the table, at the point of contact of hammer and table, the input information is passed on to the table. It is similar to a sensation received by a human body. It is just that the way this information is treated is very different. Depending on the quality and range of information, the table might break or might not break.

This brings us to a very important proposition. From the perspective of IPA, there may not be a qualitative difference between living and non-living things. It is only the degree and complexity of processors that separates them. Like non-living things, living things also do not have a choice over how a particular piece of information can be processed. A particular input information would 'find' its relevant processor, get processed by it, and along with it produce a change. Thus, there is no free will, as it is commonly understood. The free will argument is also opposed on the ground that there is no single author of all actions of a person or a self (already discussed).

So what does all of this mean? If living beings (including humans) do not have free will, what is going on in the world? Is a human being merely an advanced and complex robot, which processes information and doesn't have free will, and choice is merely an illusion? It doesn't make any sense. But why does it have to make sense? Maybe the world is like that. But let us try to speculate and probe a little further. After all, from human logic, it is bewildering. Here, an analogy can be drawn with a colony of robots interacting with each other and the environment. Why would such a system come into being? If there is a creator, why would it create something like this?

For us to understand this, we must first look at how it all started.

Let us start with an assumption that the universe is a closed system (i.e., information can neither escape the universe nor can new information enter the universe). This can be correlated with energy, but I prefer to use information. So the universe is a closed system within which information is flowing, getting processed, producing certain changes, and then again acting as input for another processor.

Now an important question to ask is how the information entered the system for the first time. We will not focus on how a particular piece of information is processed by a processor. The functioning of the universe is explained by the physical sciences like physics, chemistry, biology, etc. Here, we are more concerned about how did the information enter the system for the first time. For this, we must go back to the origin of the universe. The most accepted theory right now about this is the Big Bang theory. As it has been observed that the universe is expanding, there must have been a time when everything was together in a super condensed state called 'singularity.' There was a big explosion, and it all started from there. This explosion can be considered as the first injection of information into the system. But again, the obvious question is how did the explosion come about? If the singularity is considered as a closed system, any information cannot enter from outside. How did the system move from a state of rest to a state of motion by itself?

This is a common problem posed by theologians to scientists, and also acts as an argument to prove the existence of God, which is assumed to be the first cause or the first mover. We will try to answer this question using IPA.

Randomness

What is a truly random event? Flipping a coin to get heads or tails is not truly random because if we know variables such as the force with which a coin was flipped, the air friction, weight of the coin, hardness of the landing surface, we can determine exactly what the result would be. We are assuming that there is unlimited computational power with us.

Thus, randomness should not be linked with one's capability to predict the outcome. A truly random event would be one in which even if we have knowledge of all the variables, information, and unlimited computational power, we cannot predict the outcome of an event. Thus, in a closed system (based on the four dimensions), there cannot be a truly random event, as one can always predict the event if they are given all variables, all the information, and unlimited computational powers.

But if there is even a single truly random event, it would indicate that the system is not completely closed. I am not an expert on quantum physics, but whatever limited knowledge I have about it, at the quantum level, it can be said that things seem to work in truly random manner. In the famous double slit experiment (explaining the whole experiment is beyond the scope of this book but you can find several animations of it on youtube) if we put particle detectors on each of the two holes, one cannot predict the hole through which a particle would enter. This is thus a truly random event. It is different from Newtonian randomness. So if there is even one truly random event in the universe, it indicates that some information from outside the system has leaked into the system. As we can account for only that information, which comes from within the system, we cannot predict an event in which external information is also involved.

Quantum entanglement is one such phenomenon, which cannot be explained if the system is assumed to be closed. 'The basic idea of quantum entanglement is that two particles can be intimately linked to each other even if separated by billions of light years of space, a change induced in one will affect the other' (www.space.com). This might indicate an open system.

Now, let's go back to the Big Bang theory and the first cause which set the system rolling. It seems more plausible that the initial impetus was provided from outside the system, which would be considered a truly random event if it is seen from inside the system. The impetus coming from outside the system transgresses the body of physicalism, and thus, here we enter the metaphysical realm or the *noumena* in the language of Immanuel Kant.

Another area of inquiry where the role played by truly random variables can be seen is the theory of natural selection. Random cell-mutations play a key role in natural selection. The cell mutations that help in the survival of an organism are passed on to its off-springs. But if we are assuming mutations to be truly random, this would mean there is some information coming from outside the system. It may seem outrageous but this opens the possibility that evolution after all may not be by an accident. Here I am referring only to the mutation part. Of course, the external environment plays a key role in natural selection and thus the overall process of evolution does not *seem* completely random.

Quantum Physics is the best contender right now to explain the truly random events but it can be any other process. The basic idea is that information is flowing from outside the system into the system (i.e. the four dimensions). As we know that quantum principles work at the very fundamental level, this implies that there is a flow of information from outside the system into the system (or reverse) or at least there is a scope for it. This brings us to an interesting possibility, the possibility of this world being a simulation.

The Matrix World

In the movie 'The Matrix' the world in which the humans live is shown as a computer simulation. Could this be true? Recently Elon Musk also said that there is one in a billions chance that reality is not a simulation. In fact, the idea of world being a simulation goes back to

Shankaracharya's Advaita Vedanta (Non-Dualism). He summed up the philosophy in this line:

Brahman satyam, jagat mithya, jivo brahmaiva naparah

It means that Brahman is the only reality, the world is unreal, and there is no difference between Brahman and individual self. How can this be understood from the perspective of information?

Imagine the quantum level as the gateway of information coming from outside the system. Just as a computer software, no matter how sophisticated, is based on the binary code at the fundamental level, the complex world we see around ourselves could be based on the very basic type of information coming from the quantum gateways. What if an entity from outside the system is coding the program of this world by sending in stream of information through the quantum gateway. As the gateway of information is at such a fundamental level it would give the entity behind simulation a lot of sway to *manipulate* the system. But it is also true that the system is already so sophisticated that the entity may not have to interfere too much as the information system has already been set rolling with internal laws and mechanisms like laws of motion, principle of natural selection, etc. I end this chapter with a word of caution. Whatever is said above must be taken with a pinch of salt. The purpose here is to explore the possibilities and not give a conclusive theory.

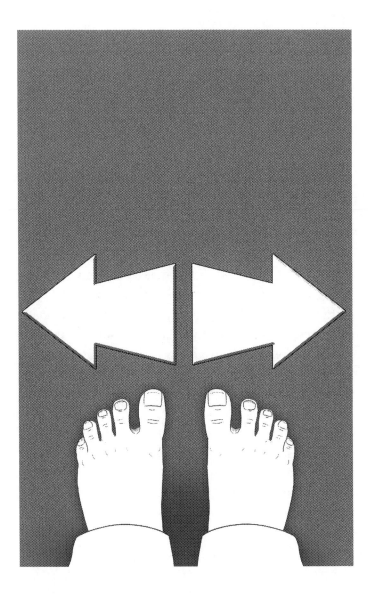

Free Will:
Determinism or Inevitability

*You say: I am not free. But I have raised
and lowered my arm. Everyone understands
that this illogical answer is an irrefutable
proof of freedom.*

—*Leo Tolstoy*

We have already discussed free will from the perspective of IPA. We came to conclusion that free will doesn't exist, as it is commonly understood. The first reason behind this is that there is no single and absolute author of actions performed. There is no 'self' as such. Also, the processors are preprogrammed to process information. Thus, there is no scope left for free will. But the open nature of universe makes things interesting.

Impact of Open Universe on Free Will

Initially, we had assumed the system to be completely closed. Thus, the principle of causation was applied in a strict sense. This not only eliminated any scope of free will; rather, it pushed things to extreme (i.e., inevitability). There is a difference between 'determined' and 'inevitable.'

Inevitable

If we know the initial state of the universe and we have an unlimited computational power, we can predict its state at any time T. This would also mean the state of any human being can be predicted, which means whatever is going to happen is already fixed. Obviously, there is no scope for free will in such a scenario. This would hold true only in a closed system.

Determined

In this case, although one still doesn't have free will, but even with unlimited computational power, the state of universe at time T cannot be predicted. Why? Because if the system is not closed, new information can enter from outside and change the course of events and would lead to a different stream of events from the one as predicted by assuming the system to be closed.

Thus, an open system still doesn't allow free will to exist, but it makes sure that nothing is inevitable. If the system is assumed to be open, it can have serious implications on theology, religion, and science.

God: Who Pressed Start?

Now, therefore, the instruction [about Brahman]: Neti, neti—not this, not this.

—Brihadaranyaka Upanishad

The idea of God is present in all culture and societies in one form or the other. It is most commonly understood, as a divine entity, which created this world including us is very powerful if not omnipotent and can interfere in our lives positively or negatively. Most of the religions across the world are centred on one or many gods, barring exceptions like Buddhism and Jainism. But there is hardly anyone who has seen or experienced God. Thus, there are several proofs for the existence of God. Most of the religions believe that God, as an entity, resides outside the system, and thus can influence the system from outside. Here, outside should not be merely understood in the spatial context. Tomorrow, if we come to know that God lives on a distant planet, it would not mean it is outside the system. The whole universe is one system; outside the system means beyond the four dimensions of space and time. So how do we see God from IPA's point of view? We understand that all the processes and changes are taking place in the system because of the flow of information. But from where did the *first information* in the system come from? Can we call the principle behind this first information as God?

God: Creator and Operator

If the 'first information' was provided from outside the system, it would mean that the system was at least initially open. If the system was initially open, it is more likely that it would be open even now. Thus, if God is considered as the phenomena behind the first information entering the system, it follows that God has not only created this world, but also keeps interfering in it. From the point of Theology, this means God has not only created the world but also operates it. The terms like God, creation, and operation should not be understood literally. In fact, the meaning they carry in this context is very different, but they help us in conveying the idea in the simplest possible way.

True Love is Random

Your task is not to seek for love, but merely to seek and find all the barriers within yourself that you have built against it.

—Rumi

God and love are the two most used, but least understood words. It would be inappropriate to blame someone for their lack of understanding because these two words can be understood at many levels, and thus could have very different meanings not just for different people, but for the same person over different times. We have already tried to understand God as a principle. You might absolutely disagree with this understanding, which is perfectly fine. After all, in understanding God, I have tacitly transgressed the system. The normal rules and laws may not apply outside the system, and thus, as the famous German philosopher Immanuel Kant said, it becomes a matter of faith and belief. Science operates within the system, and thus cannot say about, let alone prove or disprove the existence of God.

The commonly understood meaning of love entails a feeling of care and compassion for a person, thing, or idea. A mother loves her child, a husband loves his wife, a person loves his belonging, and another person loves his country. Sometimes, love is said to be a selfish act because a person cares for his object of love because he is dependent on it. Even acts of altruism are based on the principle that the person performing the act derives pleasure from it, so we are governed by the same processors discussed above. We simply act and our act is perceived as that of love based on personal beliefs and social conventions. From the perspective of IPA, it is simply the processing of information. Everyone does what he does to maximize pleasure and minimize pain. But, as discussed, if the system is not closed, there are other inputs coming from outside the system, which interact with elements of the system. Could that interaction have something to do with love?

Some of us have experienced certain events, which is difficult to explain through the laws within the system. For example, when I was staying in a boarding school, I got very sick once. I suffered from food poisoning and could not sleep the whole night. The next morning, to my surprise, I got a message from the telephone booth (at that time, there were no mobile phones, there were PCO booths) that my mother wants to speak to me urgently. After talking to her, I came to know that even she could not sleep the whole night, and was having dreams that I was very sick. This could be a mere coincidence. But there have been similar incidents in my life and other people have also narrated stories like this. I want to make it clear here, I am not supporting an anthropomorphic view of God and love. Rather, I am opposed to it. We are a speck of dust in the scheme of this vast universe, but I am talking about the possibility of existence of a principle that is beyond logic and beyond the system, but has a significant bearing on us.

There is a possibility that true random variables/ events of the universe point toward something that cannot be understood from our normal framework of knowledge. The random events might be pointing toward something, which we vaguely grasp at the subconscious level, but are not capable of controlling and manipulating it. Thus, *true love* can be understood here as something transcendental (beyond the system), and it manifests in our system through true random events. Thus, true love can be said to be random.

Also, praying to God for desired results may not seem so outlandish from the above perspective. After all, praying can be an expression of love toward the God (the principle). It might be a way to access, or maybe even influence the random events. The power of this love may depend on the profundity with which a person can connect with the other dimension. In Hindu philosophy, *bhakti marg* or the path of devotion (toward God) is considered as a potent means of attaining liberation. At a deeper level, one might be able to connect with God, which is the first mover who is outside the system, and yet can influence it and which provided the firs information to this system.

This thought closely resembles the Vedantic philosophy where Brahman is the ground of existence and is present in everything. It might be true that our true nature is not realized by most of us, and to attain it, one needs to move beyond the system. But the insight attained by historical figures like Buddha and Shankaracharya point toward the possibility of accessing what is beyond the system, and realize the true nature of reality. Existentialist philosopher, Heidegger, described humans as *Dasein* or being there. He believed that the principle of existence runs through everything, but only humans are capable of realizing it. This could be the key difference between humans and other animals and inanimate objects.

Morality: Which Way to Heaven?

> *The pendulum of the mind oscillates between sense and nonsense, not between right and wrong.*
>
> —*CG Jung*

Morality is the principle of right and wrong. If the system is considered as closed, then morality becomes completely dependent on the belief system. A belief system is a set of norms and principles in a society commonly accepted by the people living in it. In a society where virtue is valued, morality would be based on virtues. An act of honesty would be moral, whereas an act of lying would be immoral. In another society where utilitarianism is cherished, an act of murder may also be justified if it results in greater happiness for the society. I believe the concepts of right and wrong, as understood normally, are very fluid. They depend on the perception of the subject. During World War II, mass killing of Jewish people was justified by the society on outlandish grounds. Thus, as long as morality is derived from the belief system of a society, it will be very fluid and subjective. When the belief system would change, the moral laws would also change. Think of any immoral act, and I bet it can be justified in a society (if not real, hypothetical) with a certain belief system in a particular context. I am not saying this type of moral system is justified or not, this is simply the state of affairs.

If morality has its roots, not in a local belief system but in a universal principle, then the moral laws would be applicable across societies and across time. We don't know whether such a principle exists, but at least it would be theoretically consistent to say that moral laws would be absolute whatever they may be. An open universe leaves open a possibility of such an external universal principle. This particular idea of morality, based on an absolute, can be identified with the ideas in Bhagavad Gita. Krishna, during the battle of Kurukshetra, asks Arjuna to kill his brothers and relatives. When Arjuna is reluctant to do so, Krishna explains to him the universal truth. He tells Arjuna that everyone in this world has to perform actions in accordance with the *cosmic purpose*.

That is the true Dharma or duty of every individual and that is the right thing to do. This cosmic purpose here can be associated with a universal principle. Similarly, Kant's deontological theory of morality talks about duty for duty sake. One should perform an action, not for fulfilling a desire or out of fear, but for simply performing that duty. According to him, the right action is the action performed in reverence to a law. He gave examples of such laws through his categorical imperatives. We don't need to go into those right now, it is sufficient to understand that a categorical imperative is like a universal law.

Again a 'universal principle' is highly speculative. We don't know, in fact, we might never come to know about such a universal principle. So it is only good for theoretical discussions right now. For the real world, we need moral values. Otherwise, the world would collapse. These moral values could be based on the norms of the society, religion, logic, or evolutionary grounds. It is more important that people or society, as a whole, has a moral system, and it adheres to the moral rules. Otherwise, it might become a chaotic jungle. There is a separate discipline of ethics for understanding and deciding what makes an action right or wrong. I have deliberately not focused on that, rather, I was interested here in finding the source of morality.

PART III:

Authentic Life

The study and knowledge of the universe would somehow be lame and defective were no practical results to follow.

—Cicero

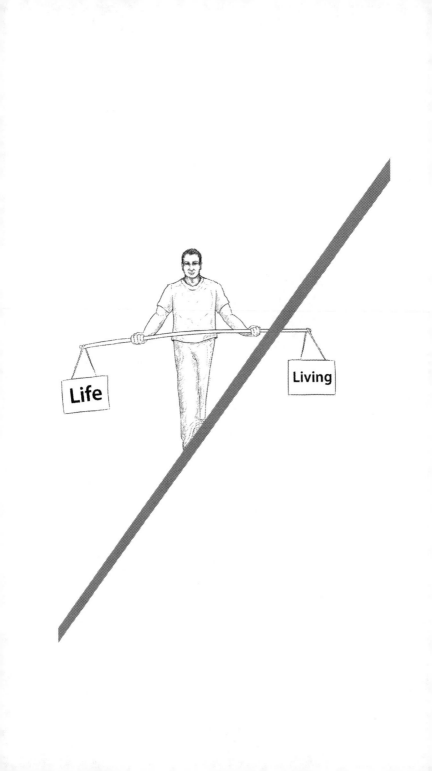

Intellectual Curiosity Versus Practical Problems of Life

Be a philosopher, but amidst all your philosophy, be still a man.

—*David Hume*

I have never shunned away from making efforts to answer the questions posed by my curios mind. I have covered some ground, but there is more to cover. Learning is a life-long process. While I am trying to answer these questions, another question often pops into my head: is it even worth trying to find answers to these questions? After all, after engaging with the fascinating world of these questions, one has to come back to the more imminent reality and its associated problems.

One has to deal in their daily lives with issues ranging from basic needs like food, clothing, and shelter to issues related to relationships, from professional success and recognition to physical discomfort one faces during illness and old age, as well as a host of other issues.

That makes me wonder whether one should be more concerned with these issues rather than wasting time in encouraging intellectual curiosity (only if one has a choice).

It is a strange double-edged sword, however, because when I am only engaged with practical issues of life, life seems incomplete; whereas when I engage myself with existential questions of life, although I enjoy the process, it seems sometimes it is merely a mental recreation (no matter how serious and important it may sound), and the daily issues of life are the real deal and I should invest my mental energy there.

Sometimes, the two realms do seem to be interconnected, and my engagement with my intellectual curiosity might yield results that may help me in daily problems of life in a better way. For example, if one feels that every person has a purpose in life and they have found their purpose, life may seem less painful and more joyous; but that is easier said than done. People who can find harmony between the two realms are indeed fortunate.

But till the time one doesn't find the right balance and harmony, life may seem chaotic and meaningless. To find order and meaning in chaos is a herculean task because till the time I find harmony, I will question my actions and thoughts making me unsure and doubtful about most of the things in the world. But it is preferable to stay in this uncertainty than to settle for a truth (whatever it maybe), which one is not convinced of. Till that time, one should keep striving for the truth and trying to strike a balance between intellectual curiosity and practical issues of life.

Mind is where the two realms meet. It is not easy to live in the world with its contingencies. Nothing can be taken for granted. Everyone has to face physical and mental challenges every day. There is physical pain, sickness, old age, and death. There is mental pain, fear, rejection, loneliness, and anxiety. A lot of factors are not in our control, but if one has control over their mind (till one can understand free will at the experiential level) at least the mental problems can definitely be dealt with in a better way. Thus, the understanding and regulation of mind can make it easier for a person in dealing with imminent problems of life, for instance, in dealing with anger.

Similarly, if one engages in intellectual curiosity, one cannot even reach close to the answers of the existential and abstract questions about life and universe if one cannot efficiently use their mental resources and faculties. For this also, one needs to understand and regulate the mind in a better way.

Thus, the common meeting ground for both seemingly contradictory realms is understanding and regulation of mind. But what do we mean by the 'understanding and regulation of mind'? Understanding here means understanding the way the mind functions and using this to regulate the mind, so that it can serve our purpose and we can have a more fulfilling life.

Information Processing Approach helps in understanding how the mind functions. We can use this understanding to regulate our minds. More specifically, through the explanation of ideas like self, consciousness, thought, and breathing, we can learn to regulate our minds.

Breathing and Thought

Using IPA, we have established that the mechanism behind thought is the processing taking place at high-level processors. We have also understood how the sensation of self is correlated to a particular thought, and also how the breathing pattern at any point is a signature of the internal state of mind (in which a thought or thoughts play a key role).

In any unpleasant situation faced by a person, the mental state plays a key role. Here, let us talk about only psychological problems and not physical ones. So for example, if a person is anxious about a job interview or afraid of an upcoming academic result, it is more to do with the mental state than the physical state. If the person understands his mind, he can regulate it to mitigate the negative feelings like fear and anxiety.

These feelings are always accompanied by thoughts. No matter how hard one tries to calm oneself by introducing other thoughts such as 'I have done this before' or 'this is no big deal,' it is difficult to shake off these negative feelings. The negative thoughts are too overpowering in this state.

As we have seen that the breathing pattern is a signature of the mental state, and thus also the thought pattern, altering the breathing pattern drastically can destabilize a negative thought. The intensity of destabilizing would depend on the strength of the ensuing thought at that particular time.

The basic idea here is that a particular thought (in this case, negative) or a set of contiguous thought requires a certain energy pattern that is reflected in the breathing pattern. Altering the breathing pattern for a while—say for ten minutes (time would depend on the intensity of negative thoughts and amount of control one has over one's mind)—can destabilize the particular negative thought because it would not get that energy pattern to survive. Meditation can help us in better regulation of our breaths and eventually the mind. But one is required to practice meditation regularly to see a long-term impact. I have discussed about the various meditative techniques later in the book. Here, I want to lay out a simple technique that can give us instant relief in times of stress and anxiety. It is based on the understanding derived from IPA. The basic idea is to disrupt the breathing pattern in times of stress.

One needs to do the following:

1) Ten slow breaths counting on each inhalation and exhalation

2) Ten fast exhalations

3) Ten medium breaths through alternating nostrils

4) Ten square breaths (count 1 to 4 on each step i.e. inhalation, holding of breath, exhalation, and holding of breath)

5) Ten quick exhalations pushing out air by applying force just below the naval

It is important to focus one's attention on one's breathing at all times. If attention gets diverted, one should not get agitated, but should simply bring one's focus back. The process takes approximately five minutes. It works for me most of the times. You can modify it to suit your needs.

One can follow a different pattern also. The basic idea is to disrupt the energy pattern associated with the negative thought pattern, so that the negative thought pattern cannot survive and one's mind is cleansed of it. Once the mind is clear of thoughts, a person has much more control over one's mind. One can use it more efficiently, and for whatever purpose one wants.

With a clear mind, I believe one is peaceful, more creative, and one's life seems less painful. It is easier to address one's intellectual curiosity as the mental resources can be efficiently used to find answers to those questions.

No matter what kind of psychological problem one faces, be it fear, anxiety, loneliness, or insecurity, instead of trying to solve the problem intellectually, if one is able to cleanse the mind of any thoughts first, one can tackle any seemingly difficult situation of life. One must focus on emptying the mind.

Relationships and the Art of Listening

When people talk, listen completely.
Most people never listen.

—*Ernest Hemingway*

When we talk about the practical aspects of life, we must talk about relationships. We are social animals, and we cannot survive in isolation. It is said that this special ability of Homo sapiens of cooperating with members of their own species in unique ways was responsible for their survival over competing species like Neanderthals. But I feel the modern day society is gradually forgetting the art of nurturing and maintaining relationships.

IPA can help improve our understanding about relationships, and a better understanding can help cultivate better relationships. The main problems faced by people in unhealthy relationships are unreasonable expectations and conflict. I have discussed both these ideas earlier in the book. If we don't understand the other person properly, it leads to unreasonable expectations and unfulfilled expectations lead to disharmony and conflict. The key to avoiding these two is the better understanding of the people around us and ourselves.

Relationships can be said to be working at three levels:

1. Relationship with ourselves
2. Relationship with family and friends
3. Relationship with society (includes professional relationships and relationship with country)

Imagine these three levels as concentric circles with *relationship with self* as the innermost circle, and *relationship with society* as the outermost circle. The innermost circle is the foundation on which second level is based, and these two combined is the foundation on which the third level is based. So if one does not have a good relationship with themselves, it may not be possible to have a good relationship with family and friends and so on. In my personal experience, the people who I have seen to share good relationships with people around them are very comfortable with themselves.

So what is the key to a good relationship at any level? I believe 'listening' is the key. Here, listening not only means the physical act of listening through ears, but it also means to let information inside our system without imposing a framework or judgement on it. At the personal level, it could mean just observing one's thoughts without labelling or passing a judgement. Similarly, when we are interacting with other people, we must listen to them patiently by being both physically and mentally present with them at that time. In common parlance, we call it talking heart to heart. Normally, we are so impatient with ourselves and others that we don't even give a chance to listen properly. In fact, it would not be an over simplification to say that meditation is listening. In ancient India, the sages used to sit near rivers and listen to sound of the gush produced by them.

Listening is an art—an endangered one. Most of us are hearing and not listening, and that could spell disaster for relationships. We must give the other person an environment, which is conducive for him to express himself without any inhibitions. That itself would bring serenity and calmness to the relationship. It would help a person understand the other person's point of view. It would help understand why that person thinks and acts in a certain way. But listening out is not easy; it requires a lot of patience and strength. But it also gives a very strong and stable foundation to any relationship be it the relationship with ourselves or relationship with others.

In fact, to love someone is to listen to them. *Loving is listening and listening is loving.* If you listen properly, you would understand the person better; and only if you understand them better that you can resolve their concerns and make them happier. There should not be any ego acting as an obstruction to the flow of information. Ego qualifies the information as good and bad, right and wrong, etc. Rather, there should be an incessant flow of information between the speaker and the listener.

Job Satisfaction: An Illusion?

(Adapted from my TED talk delivered at IIT Delhi)

We can never obtain peace in the outer world until we make peace with ourselves.

—Dalai Lama XIV

It is difficult to completely eliminate job dissatisfaction due to psychological and evolutionary reasons. It can, however, be significantly lowered if its root cause is understood well and dealt with intelligently. IPA can help us identify and understand the root cause of dissatisfaction. What follows is an attempt to establish a framework to first see how job dissatisfaction manifests itself in different scenarios. Then we will use IPA to decode it.

If I were to ask you a question, 'do you love your job?' What would you say? I bet not more than 20–30 per cent of people would reply in affirmative. That is a pretty low number but is that surprising? I don't think so. We know for a fact that most of us are not satisfied with our jobs, but why is that? Why are Monday mornings so depressing for a lot of people? Why do we feel that if we get a particular job, we will be satisfied and yet that does not happen? Why do even the best employers of the world face a high attrition rate? Job dissatisfaction is so universal, and yet we hardly try to understand the exact reason behind it. So let's try doing that.

Before proceeding further, let me tell you that in the last six years, I have been in six jobs. I therefore, have ample first-hand experience of getting dissatisfied with my job. I have worked in different roles in different organizations: startups, private companies, governmental and semi-governmental set ups, I've worked as a project officer, an analyst, a consultant, and am currently a civil servant.

During this journey, I've learnt something that I would like to share. I feel our understanding about job dissatisfaction is inadequate and merely improving our understanding can significantly lower our dissatisfaction levels, so let us try to improve our understanding.

What are the things we look for in a job? Obviously, it is very subjective. For some people, remuneration might be most important while for others job content might come first. But there are a few common ingredients which most of us look for in a job with varying degrees.

We look primarily at a few things:

- Remuneration
- Work-Life Balance
- People
- Infrastructure
- Connect with Org Goal

- Job Content
- Recognition
- Variety

This is not an exhaustive list of parameters at all. In fact, I believe there cannot be one universal list for everyone. You could have a completely different list of parameters. This is an indicative list, which will serve our purpose for now.

Now what we do is we assign a score between one and ten to all the above parameters based on how we *perceive* them. For example, if I feel my remuneration is low, I will assign it a value closer to zero (say three) and vice versa. After scoring all the parameters, we plot it on a graph and we get a spider chart like this (Illustration 23.1).

Now, a word of caution, this total score should not be seen in isolation. It should not be considered as an absolute score of your job satisfaction, but just a tool to compare levels of satisfaction across jobs.

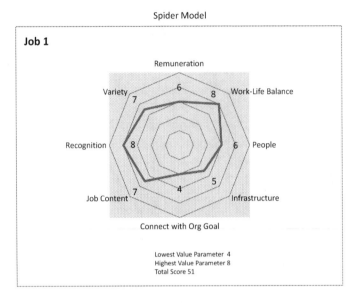

Illustration 23.1

From this spider web, we will look at the three values required for our analysis:

i) i) Lowest Value Parameter or LVP – The parameter(s) with the lowest values(s)

ii) ii) Highest Value Parameter or HVP – The parameter(s) with the highest value(s)

iii) iii) Total Score – Sum of all the scores

Now let us consider three hypothetical scenarios using the spider model

i) Scenario One – LVP

Let us imagine a situation in which a person Bob working in Job 1 is dissatisfied with his job because he does not feel connected with the organization's goal. He switches to Job 2 in which he feels more connected to the organization's goal. For some time, he feels happier in the new job. But after some time, he again becomes dissatisfied, as he has to work late hours and he is not able to strike work-life balance. Why does this happen?

The spider charts of Job 1 and Job 2 made by Bob are presented in Illustration 23.2.

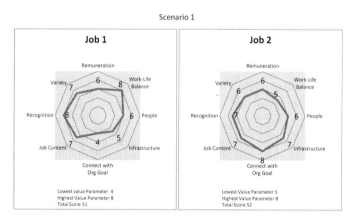

Scenario 1

Illustration 23.2

The apparent reason for Bob's dissatisfaction with Job1 is the parameter 'Connect with Organizational Goal'. It is also obvious from the spider chart as it is the Lowest Value Parameter (LVP). This leads him into switching to Job 2 where he perceives a higher score on this parameter. This is pretty intuitive. If we have less of something, we try to increase it. But the underlying functioning of mind is different. This is only the apparent reason. So what is the real reason?

The real reason for dissatisfaction is that we inherently tend to focus (emphasis) on that parameter in the spider chart whose value is the lowest (LVP) more than the other parameters, and make our choices based on that very parameter. Connect with organizational goal just happens to be the LVP in this case.

Had 'connect with organizational goal' been the real reason for dissatisfaction for him, he would have been satisfied with Job 2. But he is dissatisfied here also. It's just that the apparent reason for dissatisfaction has changed from 'connect with organizational goal' to 'work-life balance' (new LVP of 5). The real reason is the same—focus the LVP more than other parameters. Decisions based on LVP will hardly help him escape the cycle of dissatisfaction.

Another thing to note in this scenario is that the total score hasn't changed much from Job 1 to Job 2.

ii) Scenario 2 – Total Score

This scenario is not very different from the first one. Here, however, there is significant increase in total score between Job 1 and Job 2.

Bob switches to a job not just with a higher score in LPV (i.e., connect with org goal but also with a high total score, i.e., 59)—that is a jump of 16 per cent (Illustration 23.3). Here, the job dissatisfaction levels would be lower than Scenario 1 initially. But sooner or later, he will start getting bugged by his new LPV (i.e., remuneration, in this case). Here again, focus on the new LPV will become the cause of dissatisfaction. As long as our choices are determined by looking at the LPV, there will be job dissatisfaction.

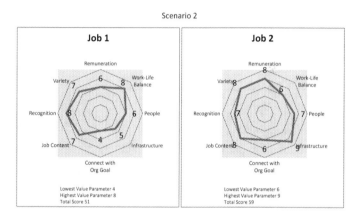

Scenario 2

Illustration 23.3

iii) Scenario 3 – Highest Score

In this scenario, Bob lands in a job where he scores at least one of the parameters as perfect ten (Illustration 23.4). Chances are high that he has found his passion. A score of ten can compensate for the LVPs, but this is not as simple as it seems. Scoring a parameter as ten means that the person feels there is no further scope for improvement on that parameter. So technically, you cannot score remuneration as ten. Similarly, it is difficult to score recognition as ten, as it depends more on external factors thus involves subjectivity. But it may be possible to score job content as ten. I am pretty sure Sachin Tendulkar and AR Rehman would have scored their job content as ten. Similarly, it could be possible to give a ten on the parameter of connect with organisational goal. I guess you got my point.

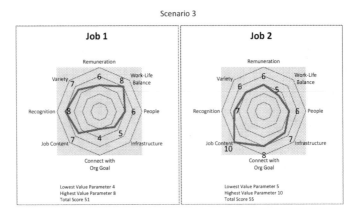

Scenario 3

Illustration 23.4

Reasons for Focusing on Low Value Parameters

We have understood that there is an apparent reason for dissatisfaction, which is the LVP and there is the real reason for dissatisfaction, which is our inherent tendency to focus on the LVP more than the other parameters and make our decisions based on that.

Now let's try delving in a little deeper, and try to understand the dynamics behind the real reason for dissatisfaction. Are we hardwired to focus more on the negatives than the positives? This is a phenomenon called *Negativity Bias*—it has been already explained earlier in the book using IPA.

Basically, we get disproportionately affected by negative feelings than positive ones. Imagine yourself in two different situations. In the first situation, you win an Rs 500 gift voucher; and in the second, you lose Rs 500 in a bet. Situation two makes you feel disproportionately bad than situation one makes you feel good. Negativity Bias is most probably an evolutionary phenomenon— negative feelings have helped in making us more aware of and avoiding danger, which has been a critical survival skill.

This was a very essential skill when we were hunters and gatherers. Today, we live in a largely secure physical environment. The kinds of dangers we face are very different, but there has been rapid change in our lifestyles in the last 2000 years or so, but our genes have not kept pace with it.

How to Deal with Job Dissatisfaction?

1. **Awareness** - Be aware about factors that determine your job dissatisfaction. Make your own spider chart and find out the LPV. This will give you clarity about the reasons for job dissatisfaction.

2. **Making Informed Decisions -** Understand the importance of the lowest score (LVP) in your spider chart, and don't take hasty decisions. Try

not to fall in the unending cycle of maximizing your LPV.

3. **10/10** - Try extending an already long vertex of the spider web even longer, so that it approaches ten. It is easier said than done, but you should keep trying. You might find your passion and break the cycle of dissatisfaction.

4. **Reprogramming your mind** – We are hardwired to think, in a particular way, focusing on the negatives. This is a very old habit, which cannot be changed overnight. In the long run, uncondition your mind and start focusing on positives rather than negatives. Meditation can be a good place to start.

The bad news is that we are somehow hardwired to dislike our jobs, so we should not be too harsh on ourselves if we are not able to find that perfect job.

The good news is that it is possible to lower dissatisfaction levels if the factors causing it are understood properly.

A Brief Survey of Common Meditation Techniques

Nowhere can man find a quieter or more untroubled retreat than in his own soul.

—Marcus Aurelius

In this book, I have talked about the importance of meditation at several instances. I have tried to explain the process underlying meditation. There are numerous meditative techniques, and a person can adopt any technique that suits them. What follows is a brief survey of basic meditative techniques. It is especially meant for people who are new to meditation.

What is meditation? For most people, the first image that comes to their minds is a person sitting in lotus position with eyes closed. But when one tries meditating, the first question that comes to the mind is that what they are supposed to do after closing their eyes. In fact, most people find it punishing to close their eyes and sit quietly for more than five minutes. The answer to that question is not simple. Therefore, there are many versions of it given by different people.

The different versions translate into different techniques of meditation. They do not necessarily answer the question 'what is meditation?' The road that leads to Srinagar cannot be equated with Srinagar itself. The techniques are not answers themselves, but they definitely help us in getting close to the answer to our question. At the cost of a little oversimplification, most meditative techniques can be identified with three stages: purification, concentration, and insight.[1] Purification means relieving our mind from external and internal distractions. Concentration refers to focusing our mind on a particular entity. Insight means achieving the highest level of concentration where the duality between subject and object disappears.

People across cultures, over the years, have developed several meditation techniques. This shows the universal nature of humans to practice meditation. Although the meditative experience may start differently under various techniques, but with later stages, it starts converging toward a common point. Still, it is important to get familiar with the different techniques. They can be classified into the following categories (these are not watertight as there is significant overlapping between them).

Types of Meditative Techniques

1. Concentration Technique

In this technique, the subject starts concentrating on a particular entity. It could be a physical object, a thought or his breath. Most commonly, the subject concentrates on his breath. Every time his mind digresses, he is supposed to bring his concentration back. Counting the breaths every time he breathes in and breathes out helps in maintaining the concentration. It is not as easy as it sounds. It requires a lot of mental energy. Thus, the mind with all its energy channelized at one place withdraws itself from all external and internal distractions. Eventually, the duality between the breather and the breath disappears. Schools like Patanjali Yoga and Art of Living (Sudarshan Kriya) employ this technique.

2. Mantra Repetition

In this technique, an abstract phrase is recited repetitively by the subject. The phrase is uttered in coordination with the breaths. A very popular phrase is '*so hum.*' As the subject breathes in, he says 'so,' and when he breathes out, he says 'hum'. Practising it for about twenty minutes can help channelize his mental energy. A very important point to be noted here is that it can be any phrase as long as it does not carry a meaning. If the phrase has a meaning, the mind would start pondering over it and the whole purpose of meditation would be defeated. Schools like Transcendental Meditation follow this technique.

3. Neutral Observation of Mind

In this technique, the subject, after a few minutes of breathing exercise, starts observing the contents in his mind. The idea here is to observe the thoughts and feelings without any bias. Just as a person sitting in a garden watches birds coming and disappearing in the sky without getting affected, the subject should observe his thoughts and feelings emanating from his mind without getting affected by them. It does not come easily, but is definitely possible with some practice. Gradually, the subject realizes that the thoughts are impermanent in nature. If the mind is attentive (mindful), it can realize the true nature of thoughts and not get affected by them. Schools like Vipassana and Zen Buddhism use this technique.

4. Seeking the Truth

This is not strictly a technique, but still deserves attention. In our daily lives, we encounter some very complex questions. An honest effort toward seeking the answers, and eventually the truth, channelizes the mental energies to one point. For example, trying to answer a simple question like 'what is fear?' or 'why do we fear?' can lead us to the inner realms of our minds.

5. Mindfulness

It is a state of being attentive to the present. Although all the above techniques include mindfulness, they do not cover it entirely. The writings of Thich Nhat Hahn, the famous Buddhist monk has popularised this technique more than anything else. We don't need to be necessarily sitting in a lotus position. One can practice mindfulness even while washing dishes or taking a walk. The key here is to be exactly aware of what we are doing every moment. Therefore, for some people dancing is a form of meditation, as they are fully present there when dancing. Similarly, playing an instrument, writing, painting, etc. can also be forms of meditation if done earnestly in the right spirit.

Why Meditate?

There is a famous Zen story in which a person is riding his horse on a trail in full speed. Another person walking on the trail asks him, 'Where are you going in such a hurry?' The man replies 'I have no idea, ask the horse.' This story accurately depicts the state of affairs today. The mind has taken control over us. We have become its slave. Most of us don't even realize what we are doing at a given moment. People getting hooked to their mobile phone screens is a perfect example of how our mind dictates our actions. There is nothing wrong in looking at those screens (except that the prolonged exposure of photons emitted can damage our eyes). The problem lies in the fact that we do so inadvertently. We should be mindful of what we are doing.

This has led to lack of control over our lives. We often indulge in activities merely to escape the present. We are preoccupied with the past, and too concerned about the future. We are not able to communicate properly with ourselves and people around us. This creates misunderstanding, which leads to negative feelings like hatred, jealousy, and greed. We don't want to face ourselves because that makes us uncomfortable. We always try to seek peace and happiness outside whereas they can only be found inside us.

There is no paucity of articles in popular print media stating the benefits of meditation. It keeps our mind healthy, makes us attentive, brings peace and joy, improves our efficiency, relaxes our mind, etc.

Where to start?

One can choose any of the techniques, which suit them the most, but it should not be imposed on oneself by an external force. The inner urge is key to sustain the practice of meditation. One should not meditate to achieve a short-term goal. It should be a way of life. It is the nature of mind to meditate. Daniel Goleman's book is aptly titled *Meditative Mind*. One does not need to try too hard, he just needs to open that already existing door within him.

Meditation is a subjective experience. In spite of numerous techniques, every person is bound to shape his own unique method, while traversing into his mental realms. Therefore, there is no right or wrong way. The only requirement is that the person should have utmost humility. He should avoid having any bias or prejudice. Where there is humility, there can be infinite possibilities.

References for A brief survey of common meditative techniques

1. *The Meditative Mind: The Varieties of Meditative Experience* by Daniel Goleman

Printed in the United States
By Bookmasters